THE FOUNDATIONS OF AMERICAN LAW

THE

FOUNDATIONS

OF

AMERICAN LAW

A Companion to the 1L Year

H. Jefferson Powell

PROFESSOR OF LAW

DUKE UNIVERSITY SCHOOL OF LAW

CAROLINA ACADEMIC PRESS

Durham, North Carolina

LIBRARY OF CONGRESS CATALOGING-IN-PUBLICATION DATA

Names: Powell, Jefferson, 1954- author.
Title: The foundations of American law : a companion to the 1L year / H. Jefferson Powell.
Description: Durham, North Carolina : Carolina Academic Press, LLC, 2024. | Includes bibliographical references and index.
Identifiers: LCCN 2023053876 | ISBN 9781531029517 (paperback) | ISBN 9781531029524 (ebook)
Subjects: LCSH: Law--United States--History. | Law--United States--English influences. | Practice of law--United States--History. | Common law--United States.
Classification: LCC KF380 .P685 2024 | DDC 349.73--dc23/eng/20231201
LC record available at https://lccn.loc.gov/2023053876

CAROLINA ACADEMIC PRESS
700 Kent Street
Durham, North Carolina 27701
(919) 489-7486
www.cap-press.com

Printed in the United States of America

For Julian (born 1/19/2022) and Avalon (6/5/2013–10/19/2020)
With love and hope

Contents

Acknowledgments

This book's immediate origins lie in a series of lectures I gave to first-year law students a number of years ago. More generally, the book is the product of many years trying to teach 1L classes: as is always the case, the students have taught the teacher in countless ways. I am grateful to them all.

Several of my colleagues attended the lectures. Many thanks to each of them, and particularly to Barak Richman for his painstaking attention, and to Curt Bradley and Neil Siegel for independently suggesting that the lectures might be the basis for a book.

Three members of my family patiently listened to each lecture as I practiced it. I benefitted greatly from the comments, criticism, and encouragement of my wife Sarah and my older daughter Sara.

The book is dedicated to two whom I love.

Avalon, our Doberman, was the third member of that family practice audience. She was indeed patient, but she made no comments on the substance: being a wise dog, she no doubt thought the entire affair simply one more example of how strange human beings are. Sarah and I miss her joyful presence every day.

The birth of our grandson Julian has enriched us immeasurably. There are no words to describe the wonder of having such a bright and loving spirit in our lives.

THE FOUNDATIONS OF AMERICAN LAW

Introduction

For well over a century, the signature form of American legal education has involved the casebook and "Socratic" dialogue. Rather than having students read a text that explains whatever subject is being taught, and then attend lectures further explaining what they've read, American law teachers have insisted that the students infer the substance of whatever general area of law they're supposed to be learning by reading specific cases, and then explain the law to the professor. While this rather odd form of instruction no longer dominates the upper two years in American law schools, it remains typical of first-year "doctrinal," subject-matter defined, courses.

The pedagogy adopted in 1L classes is not a trivial matter. The first year in law school is (or ought to be) an immersion in the modes of speech and thought that constitute the American legal tradition. The old cliché about learning how to think like a lawyer is wrong only in that it makes the process sound overly cerebral: entering into the legal tradition involves adopting a worldview with emotional and even perceptual elements in addition to specifically intellectual ones. What the 1L year demands of students is more like learning to speak another language than it is akin to absorbing information in an introductory history or biology course. Furthermore, everything a law student does in the two subsequent years, indeed everything that individual does in the rest of a professional career in the law, builds on the foundations laid in the first year of law school. A great deal rides, therefore, on way the 1L classes are taught.

Leaving aside the questionable habit of blaming Socrates, I think the casebook/classroom dialogue model is an appropriate way of teaching a

1L doctrinal course. My reason has to do with the analogy I just drew between the first-year experience and the process of learning a modern foreign language. Instruction in an ancient, "dead" language often seeks primarily for the students to acquire passive knowledge of the language, the ability to read it but not necessarily to write or speak it. In contrast, students usually learn a modern language precisely so that they can speak and write as well as understand it; they must develop an active knowledge of the language. Professional education in American law is necessarily aimed at developing the students' active knowledge of the law because a passive understanding of information about law is professionally useless. The inductive method of requiring students to wrestle with actual cases and to articulate their understanding of what they're read in actual dialogue with the instructor is well-suited to assist the students in developing an active knowledge of what they are studying. They learn to speak the language of the law, not just to know the definitions of legal concepts.

That said, the value of a fundamentally inductive approach to the first-year doctrinal classes in law school does not require that the students infer *everything*. There is a certain amount of information about themes and ideas in American law that can be highly valuable to the process of students acquiring an active knowledge of how to think and speak as a lawyer, but that need not be communicated indirectly. I am not speaking now of the substance of legal rules and doctrines, which is not my concern in this book, but of information about how American lawyers think about and with legal principles and rules and doctrines. The kind of information I am talking about can be directly offered to the 1L student, thereby enhancing his or her ability to understand the assigned cases and other materials, and to participate meaningfully in classroom discussion. This book attempts to do just that, to inform the reader of what, speaking personally, I wish someone had simply told me in my first year of law school, rather than leaving it to me to pick up the information, sometimes years later.

The book's origins lie in a series of lectures I gave fall-semester 1L students a number of years ago, although much of the book's contents are new or extensively rewritten. I have tried to retain the flavor of oral lectures, however, because that seemed consistent with how I understand what I am trying to do—to share my personal sense of how the language of American law and lawyering works, and to explain some fundamental ideas and ways of thinking that competent lawyers are more likely to assume than to discuss. As that ambition suggests, the readers I have principally in mind are first-year law students. But I hope that the book will also be of value to people thinking about attending law school or simply interested in understanding more about American law.

Chapter one introduces the basic perspective from which I present the rest of the book. American law is, among other things, a tradition of thought and practice, and like any such tradition it is deeply shaped by its history. Many aspects of American legal thought that might seem strange make sense when we understand how they came to be. Chapter two discusses certain key ways in which the pre-Revolutionary English common-law background decisively influenced American law from Independence on, while chapter three examines the development of American legal thought from the founding era through the early twentieth century. Neither chapter is an essay in legal history; my concern in each is not to provide an historical narrative but to show the reader the ways in which important aspects of twenty-first century legal thought were formed by historical experience. Chapter four examines a series of assumptions that characterize modern American legal thought, and chapter five discusses the methods contemporary lawyers use in deploying legal concepts and legal authorities to answer legal questions. In the conclusion I address the despairing (or cynical) charge that the law is morally empty, and I discuss the moral dignity of American law and American lawyering. The endnotes following the conclusion are short essays that provide additional information on a few persons and topics that may be of interest to some readers but that would be a digression from the main line of discussion.

A great lawyer once wrote that "responsibility to reason, even technical reason, is the soul of the art of law."[1] The first year in American law schools is devoted to introducing the language and reason that are the means by which the art of American law is practiced. The goal of this book is to enhance the reader's understanding of what that 1L year is all about.

---

1. Charles L. Black, Jr., *The Humane Imagination* 26 (1986).

ONE

The Life of the Law

On November 23, 1880, a thirty-nine-year-old Boston lawyer named Oliver Wendell Holmes stood up to begin the first of a series of twelve evening lectures on the history and theory of the English common law. The lectures were sponsored by the Lowell Institute, which one historian has called "a leading New England dispenser of culture" in that era. The invitation to deliver them, as Holmes later wrote, "changed the whole course of [his] life."[1] The lectures were extremely well-attended; in their book form, Holmes's lectures became an important turning-point in the history of American legal thought, as well as the catalyst for Holmes's rapid transition from practitioner to Harvard professor (very briefly) to justice on the highest Massachusetts court and then, twenty years after that, to a seat on the United States Supreme Court.[2]

But all of this was in the future that November evening, and what is important to us at the moment is the way Holmes began that first lecture.

1. Liva Baker, *The Justice from Beacon Hill* 252 (1991).

2. Justice Holmes plays an important role in this book, in part because he played a significant historical role in shaping the tradition of American law that is the book's subject, but still more because he often stated memorably ideas that are generally shared by American lawyers. We are *not* looking to find in Holmes a hero (or a villain). Commentators have sharply differed in their views of him. A would-be biographer (who ultimately abandoned the project in despair) described Holmes as "a strange, enigmatic figure... savage, harsh, and cruel, a bitter and lifelong pessimist" while a famous federal judge once wrote that Holmes "wasn't perfect; he was only great [and characterized by] Tolerance, largeness of spirit, scientific curiosity, and liberalism in its most cosmopolitan form." For the purposes of this book, it doesn't matter what you or I think about him as a person. See the endnote for more.

"The life of the law has not been logic: it has been experience."[3]

In beginning this first chapter with Holmes's words, I mean to identify the general perspective from which we shall consider the study of American law. There are, of course, other perspectives. It would make perfect sense, for some purposes, to begin our study with a review of the American Republic's twenty-first century legal institutions, or a summary of the substance of the law those institutions administer. However, for the reasons given in the introduction, we shall approach American law as a practice, an activity, something that people do. And any such practice or activity will have a history, and its present-day shape *in practice* will embody that history, and the experience of those who practice it. Theories about what the practice should be, or even intellectual outlines of what it supposedly is, are given reality by their embodiment in past and present experience.

The life of the law has not been logic... Holmes meant for the first part of his sentence to be startling, a little shocking. In 1880, the law was usually thought of—by lawyers at any rate!—as sensible, rational, and logical, and there is a real sense in which this remains true for any serious practicing lawyer today. The connections between law and logical reasoning have deep roots in the history of our legal tradition. As we shall see, medieval and early modern English lawyers often said that the law *is* reason. Come forward a few hundred years, and you can find the Supreme Court of the United States upholding the constitutionality of a federal law because, in the Court's view, the basis of the law was "entirely reasonable;" the Court's judgment, the justices made clear, would have been different if they had regarded the law as "arbitrary or without a reasonable basis."[4] Law *should be*, or even *must be*, reason.

Holmes himself was no irrationalist. Indeed, he often referred to the law as a calling for thinkers, and he remarked in another famous lecture he gave in 1897 that "the training of lawyers is a training in logic... analogy, discrimination, and deduction." Unthinking adherence to history and tradition was no part of Holmes's mindset. "It is revolting to have no better reason for a rule of law than that so it was laid down in the time of

---

3. *The Common Law* (1881), excerpted in *The Essential Holmes* 237 (Richard A. Posner ed. 1992). Whenever possible, citations for Holmes's writings will be to *The Essential Holmes*, which is a brilliantly selected and easily accessible anthology.

4. *United States v. Kebodeaux*, 570 U.S. 387, 396 (2013).

Henry IV." The best reason for studying the history of the law, Holmes insisted, is to acquire "an enlightened skepticism" about "the worth" of what we have inherited from that history, from our experience.[5]

The life of the law... has been experience. My purpose in this chapter and the next two is to not to talk about English or American legal history for their own sake, in the way that we might discuss the reign of the Emperor Basil II and his legislative effort to protect peasant freeholders against aristocratic depredations. Anglo-American legal history *is* fascinating (for that matter so is Basil II![6]) but this book is not an essay in history. Our objective in these chapters is to look not at what is locked in the past, however interesting. Instead, we will examine what underlies the present, the foundations of American law and legal institutions as they exist in the twenty-first century, and as you and I want and need to understand those foundations if we are concerned to understand what is of practical importance in the law today. Such an understanding is equally vital if we wish to know how we might make a difference in the future. Holmes was right; the life of the law has been experience; as a result, learning something about the Anglo-American legal experience gives us an invaluable path into a deep and pragmatically useful view of the American law of today and tomorrow.

A minute after he threw out his "not logic but experience" line in November 1880, Holmes asserted that

> The law embodies the story of a nation's development through many centuries, and it cannot be dealt with as if it contained only the axioms and corollaries of a book of mathematics. In order to know what it is, we must know what it has been, and what it tends to become.[7]

I would amend Holmes's assertion only to say that twenty-first century law in the United States embodies the story not just of this nation's development but that of England before it. Again and again, when you look closely at some foundational concept, or principle, or institution in the

5. Holmes, The Path of the Law (1897), in *The Essential Holmes* 170.

6. Basil II was a medieval Roman (Byzantine) emperor, who was senior emperor 976–1025. *See The Land Legislation of the Macedonian Emperors* 111–32 (Eric McGeer trans. 2000) (introducing and providing the text of a 996 C.E. law).

7. Holmes, *The Common Law*, in *The Essential Holmes* 237.

contemporary United States, you will find signs of its origin in the royal courts of medieval England, or discover that the idea or institution was decisively shaped by the social forces at work in the nineteenth century industrialization of both countries. What the idea or institution has been is a clue, a vital one, to what it is and may become.

Let's look at one of the broadest concepts of all—the common law. Holmes titled the book into which he turned his 1880 lectures *The Common Law*, and you will encounter that expression many, many times in the next three academic years. But what do the words actually mean? About half-way through my first fall semester in law school I read a case in which a judge referred to "a court of common law" . . . and I realized I had no clear idea what he meant by that. Part of my confusion, though I didn't know it at the time, came from the fact that the expression has many meanings. What makes sense of the seven ways we use the term "the common law" is historical experience.

(1) Let's start with the strictly historical meaning of "the common law." The expression is the label universally given to the legal system that arose in the royal courts in medieval England, and that began to emerge in the reign of Henry II in the twelfth century (1154–89), although in the past common lawyers sometimes claimed more remote origins for it, attributing its essence, romantically but quite ahistorically, to the free law of the Anglo-Saxons before William the Conqueror and "the Norman Yoke." Shortly before the American Revolution, Sir William Blackstone (an English judge and the first university professor of common law) defined the common law as "the *lex non scripta*, or unwritten law . . . that collection of maxims and customs, which is now known by the name of the common law . . . probably, as a law *common* to all the realm."[8]

Despite some controversy in the early Republic, after Independence American courts generally continued to follow and develop further the English common law of property, contract, tort, and crime. They also maintained such characteristic institutional features of the English common law as grand and petit (trial) juries made up of ordinary citizens,

---

8. 1 Blackstone, *Commentaries on the Laws of England* *63, *67 (1765). Blackstone's treatise, published in four volumes 1765–1769, quickly became the classic summary of English public and common law as they existed at what turned out to be the brink of the American Revolution.

the writ of habeas corpus, and the practice of judges explaining their decisions through opinions (the usual English term is "judgments"). And of central importance to learning and understanding twenty-first century American law, founding-era Americans generally assumed that the distinctive methods of legal argument and reasoning they inherited from the practices of the royal courts and the English bar should carry over in the post-Independence state and federal legal systems. The common law in this primary historical sense thus refers to a legal method—"the common law of case-by-case reasoning and the establishment of precedent"—as much as to the substantive legal rules ascertained and applied through that method.[9]

(2) We also refer to "the common law" as opposed to "the civil law," meaning two distinct legal traditions and two different families of legal jurisdictions. England and Wales, North Carolina, and for many purposes the Republic of India are common law jurisdictions. Scotland, Louisiana, and the Republic of Angola are civil law jurisdictions. Some jurisdictions, among them Scotland and Louisiana, are really hybrids.

The historical explanation for this use of the term follows straight from meaning number 1. Common law prevails in most places that England has ruled, and nowhere else. English law displaced the native legal traditions of Wales and Ireland in the medieval and early modern eras, and the common law followed British colonialism in later times. The "civil law" is in force in all other jurisdictions that use a legal system with origins in Western Europe. Not all of these are European, or European-colonized countries (Japan, for example), but all of them have law codes that are rooted, ultimately, in Roman law as it was codified under the Emperor Justinian in the sixth century and rediscovered in northern Italy in the late eleventh.

The most striking difference between common law and civil law is often thought to be that in common law jurisdictions, the "judgments" or "opinions" issued by courts are primary legal authorities, while in civil law jurisdictions a written code enacted as legislation is dominant. The characteristic feature of common law legal systems is thus said to be the absence of a master code of laws. There is no common law equivalent to

9. *Parratt v. Taylor*, 451 U.S. 527, 531 (1981).

Justinian's Code and its modern descendants, and that absence identifies those systems as common law.

It is easy to overstate this contrast. In all contemporary common law countries, most legal disputes are governed, in part or whole, by legislation (or legislation-like regulations issued by administrators), and the legislation is very often collected and rationalized in codes. In parallel fashion, the decrees and judgments of courts and supranational tribunals such as the European Courts of Justice and of Human Rights play important practical roles in modern civil law jurisdictions. Furthermore, common law and civil law have repeatedly borrowed from one another historically, and the ever-expanding importance of the global market exerts great pressure on most countries to facilitate international commerce by allowing a convergence in the principles and procedures followed in their national legal systems. You are likely, for example, to encounter the UN-sponsored Convention on Contracts for the International Sale of Goods, a treaty that functions as a code governing such contracts that has been ratified by ninety-five countries at the time I write.

Nevertheless, there are unmistakable, systemic differences between common law and civil law that make understanding this distinction of enduring value. The most important of these differences lies in the differing visions that common and civil lawyers bring to their task. We will return to the common law vision below, in different contexts, but to summarize how it contrasts with that of the civil lawyer: when a common lawyer thinks about how to answer a legal question, her impulse is likely to begin by asking what the courts have said that's relevant. In contrast, a civil lawyer will ask which code provisions govern the answer.

(3) A very different contrast is intended when someone distinguishes "common law" from "equity." Once again, though, history provides the explanation. Medieval England contained a remarkable variety of legal systems. Alongside the common law developing in the royal courts and local tribunals of various kinds observing customary law, there were admiralty courts enforcing what we would now call the international law of the sea and naval conflict, and the courts Christian administering the Church's canon law. But over time the most important of these alternative systems was what became known as "equity," the justice administered by the Lord Chancellor.

From the Norman Conquest on, the chancellor was one of the highest officials in the *curia regis*, the king's "court," originally meaning the assembly of clerical and lay councilors gathered around the monarch to assist him in all facets of his governance, including his role as the fount of justice. By the late thirteenth century the courts of King's Bench and Common Pleas had emerged as tribunals with distinct judges and increasingly a distinctive body of procedural and substantive law—what we know as the common law. But the king's delegation of his ordinary adjudicative authority to the courts did not deprive him of the power to see that justice was done regardless of legal forms, and during the long reign of Edward III (1327–77), the chancellor's role in administering this extraordinary authority was formalized. Although the court of Chancery eventually developed rules and procedures as complex and sometimes even more rigid than the common law's, the hallmark of the chancellor's jurisprudence was said to be his discretion, as the king's conscience, to do equity.

After centuries of parallel development, usually through distinct courts, common law and equity have largely merged in contemporary Anglo-American systems. Separate courts of equity exist only in a very few states today, but the distinction between law and equity lives on in American law. There continue to be various distinctions, substantive and procedural, between "legal" and "equitable" claims and remedies. In civil cases, the most basic remedial difference is that the ordinary remedy "at law" is an award of money damages, while the paradigmatic remedy "in equity" is an injunction, a judicial order that someone do or not do something. As for procedure, traditionally, common law courts sat with juries in both civil and criminal cases. Although the civil jury has almost entirely disappeared in England and Wales, in the United States, the common law/equity distinction affects the availability of a lay jury in civil cases, largely because the Seventh Amendment and most state constitutions create a right to a jury in cases involving what are, traditionally or by analogy, common law claims or remedies.

(4) The contrast between "common law" legal principles announced through judicial decisions and the rules of law promulgated in constitutional provisions, statutes, or other legislative and administrative documents—what lawyers used to call, not altogether logically, "the written law"—is another meaning with which the term "common law" is used

in American law. In its narrower sense, this distinction draws attention to the source of the principle or rule in question and thus to its place in the hierarchy of legal authorities. Common law is the law that judges make on the basis of the judicial power understood to include what is substantively a power to legislate, but only in subordination to the legislature's constitutional authority to make law. Put another way, an act of Congress or the state legislature displaces a judge-made common law rule. Unlike the state courts, federal courts do not have a general power to make common law.[10]

In a broader sense, "common law" as an adjective can be used to characterize an area of law in which the operative rules have been overwhelmingly shaped by the courts rather than set out in the "written" authority that is its theoretical basis. For example, the oldest federal statute regulating monopoly business practices, the Sherman Antitrust Act of 1890, is sometimes referred to as a "common-law statute" because "from the beginning" Congress "expected the courts to give shape to the statute's broad mandate by drawing on common-law tradition," and specifically by adapting the act's practical application in accordance with the current and evolving understanding of "monopoly."[11] Similarly, although a number of state legislatures have codified (enacted as statutes) the common law tort of defamation (libel and slander), doing so appears usually to have a minimal effect on the freedom those states' courts exercise in continuing to develop defamation law in a common law fashion. The law of defamation in those states is nominally based on the statutes but as a functional matter decision making usually proceeds by

10. There is no federal common law of crimes, and the federal courts' authority to create rules in non-criminal cases is limited to areas of law in which there is a special federal governmental interest—for example, the law governing federal government contracts—and to admiralty and maritime law, where the authority has been inferred from the Constitution's grant to federal courts of jurisdiction in such cases. As is also true of the procedural rules that all federal courts are authorized to adopt, federal common law and judge-made admiralty law can be displaced by acts of Congress.

The extent to which state courts theoretically can and as a practical matter do engage (explicitly) in making common law, as opposed to making marginal adjustments to existing rules, varies widely among states. By the way, please don't put too much weight on the distinction I just drew between explicitly making a new rule and adjusting an existing one—we're talking about a spectrum of judicial decision making over most of which courts do not explicitly concede that they are making new law.

11. *Leegin Creative Leather Prod., Inc. v. PSKS, Inc.*, 551 U.S. 877, 899 (2007); *Nat'l Soc. of Pro. Engineers v. United States*, 435 U.S. 679, 688 (1978).

common law reasoning rather than by construing the legislature's wording.[12] More generally, the older a statute and the broader its terms, the more particular issues are likely to be settled by applying the judicial precedents addressing its construction rather than by interpreting the text independently. More on this in chapter five.

Perhaps the most striking—or puzzling—use of "common law" is with regard to the law of the United States Constitution. In terms of the hierarchy of sources of law in the overall American system, the federal Constitution lies at the opposite extreme from judge-made law. The latter gives way to "written law"—the enactments of Congress or the state legislatures, and even administrative regulations based on statutes. The Constitution, in contrast, is the written law *par excellence*: it is a document—actually a set of documents, the oldest and by far longest part of which was written in the summer of 1787 by "the Framers" meeting in Philadelphia. And that set of documents was adopted through processes that our legal system treats as expressing the will of We the People of the United States. As a consequence, the Constitution's rules of law take precedence over and displace *any and all* conflicting rules of law derived from any other source, including acts of Congress and exercises of the president's constitutional powers. There seems no place for a judge-made "common law" of the Constitution.

And yet in practice most arguments and decisions about what the federal Constitution requires or prohibits turn primarily on the decisions of the United States Supreme Court, and those decisions in turn are driven most often by the scope and implications of earlier Supreme Court precedents. As a distinguished legal scholar once wrote, "American constitutional adjudication in the Supreme Court seems a central case of common law methodology."[13] At one time, this fact-about-the-legal-world was generally uncontroversial, but in recent decades a fierce debate has raged over the weight and even the legitimacy of common law modes of reasoning in constitutional law, a normative question that

---

12. *See, e.g., Eason Publications v. Atlanta Gazette, Inc.*, 141 Ga. App. 321, 323 (1977) ("We believe the legislature when it adopted Code § 105-701 [defining libel] (which first appears in the 1863 Code) intended Georgia's law of defamation to be consistent with that of the common law.").

13. Frederick Schauer, Is the Common Law Law?, 77 Calif. L. Rev. 455, 470 n. 41 (1989).

we need not answer in seeking to understand the idea of "common law."[14] We will return to this debate in chapter four.

(5) Another common use of the term "the common law" is in reference to a specific body or bodies of law—paradigmatically, property, contracts, and torts, and to a great extent criminal law, in short, the great first-year courses on the substance of the law. Historically, these areas of law were primarily shaped by judges, and despite the vast importance of statutes in the modern era they retain much of their nineteenth and early twentieth century judge-made substance.

An important point: we often speak and think and teach the common law in these areas in the singular—in the first year you typically learn the common law of option contracts or the common law of criminal attempts or the common law governing property interests in fee simple absolute, not Arizona's law of option contracts or Pennsylvania's definition of criminal attempts. In other words, we speak and teach and study as if there were a single common law... and when we do that we echo the eventual success of the English common law courts at imposing a single law common to the entire kingdom in the medieval and early modern eras, a law that was then carried over, more or less as a whole, by the young American Republic's courts into their own decision making.

However understandable from an historical perspective, this habit is potentially misleading. From an important and for practical purposes a potentially decisive perspective, there is no longer a single common law of anything. Justice Holmes was the great critic of what he called the "subtle fallacy" of talking about "the common law," singular.

---

14. *Compare Nw. Airlines, Inc. v. Transp. Workers Union of Am., AFL-CIO*, 451 U.S. 77, 95 (1981) (opinion for a unanimous Court) ("it is much too late to deny that there is a significant body of federal law that has been fashioned by the federal judiciary in the common-law tradition.... Broadly worded constitutional and statutory provisions necessarily have been given concrete meaning and application by a process of case-by-case judicial decision in the common-law tradition.") *with Gamble v. United States*, 139 S. Ct. 1960, 1985 (2019) (Thomas, J., concurring) ("decisions made by the People—that is, to the original understanding of the relevant legal text—... may not align with decisions made by the [Supreme] Court.... Considerations beyond the correct legal meaning... are inapposite. In our constitutional structure, our role of upholding the law's original meaning is reason enough to correct course" when the Court's decisions diverge from that meaning.).

> Books written about any branch of the common law treat it as a unit, cite cases from [the United States Supreme] Court, from the Circuit Courts of Appeal, from the State Courts, from England and the Colonies of England indiscriminately, and criticise them as right or wrong according to the writer's notions of a single theory. It is very hard to resist the impression that there is one august corpus... a transcendental body of law outside of any particular State but obligatory within it unless and until changed by statute.... But there is no such body of law. The fallacy and illusion that I think exist consist in supposing that there is this outside thing to be found.... The common law so far as it is enforced in a State, whether called common law or not, is not the common law generally but the law of that State existing by the authority of that State without regard to what it may have been in England or anywhere else.

"The common law is not a brooding omnipresence in the sky, but the articulate voice of some sovereign or quasi sovereign that can be identified."[15] In other words, for Holmes there is nothing we can rightly call *the* common law of contracts, but only the contract law, whether found in statutes or judicial decisions, of England and Wales or North Carolina or the Republic of India. As long as the common law was confined to England, it was singular—in Holmes's words, the articulate voice of the English sovereign. In today's world, with many distinct "common law" jurisdictions that owe no legal allegiance to a single sovereign, there are many common laws, one for each distinct common law system. The Supreme Court adopted Holmes's view in 1938, and it is a basic presupposition of twenty-first century American law.[16]

But this raises a question about your 1L experience. If there is no brooding omnipresence in the sky, no transcendent body of contract or tort or property law—if there is no singular "common law," why do your

---

15. *Black & White Taxicab & Transfer Co. v. Brown & Yellow Taxicab & Transfer Co.*, 276 U.S. 518, 533–34 (1928) (Holmes, J., dissenting); *Southern Pacific Co. v. Jensen*, 244 U.S. 205, 222 (1917) (Holmes, J. dissenting).

16. *Erie Railroad Co. v. Tompkins*, 304 U.S. 64, 79 (1938) (quoting Holmes's dissent in *Black & White Taxicab*: "The fallacy underlying... is made clear by Mr. Justice Holmes.").

common law casebooks act as if there were? Is your 1L faculty in the grip of Holmes's "subtle fallacy?"

I don't think so. I accept as correct Holmes's attack on the brooding omnipresence, and I think the great majority of your teachers do as well...but I also believe it makes perfect sense to teach the first-year "common law" courses as unified fields of law—as the law of property in the United States, for example, rather than the property law of Vermont or South Dakota. To see why, we need to think about yet another sense in which people talk about "the common law."

(6) Maybe the common law is no brooding omnipresence, no single body of law that lies both within and beyond the borders and the authority of Vermont or South Dakota, but that doesn't mean that Vermont's property law is totally different from South Dakota's. In fact, the opposite is almost certainly true: with occasional disagreements on specific issues, Vermont and South Dakota probably have more or less the same law of property (and contract and tort and even criminal law). Where they do disagree, each state is likely to have lined up with one of the very small number of competing views each of which is shared by some other American states, and possibly some other common law jurisdictions as well. In the United States alone there are at least fifty different "common laws" in Holmes's sense (49 states and District of Columbia, leaving aside civil law Louisiana), and yet on almost all common law questions there are probably fewer than four distinct answers, and sometimes only one, in the 49 states and DC. (And surprisingly, even Louisiana at times.[17])

How can this be so? The answer has two parts. The first is that there are strong economic, social, and professional pressures pushing towards legal uniformity across state borders, and institutionalized means for developing and promoting shared answers to common law questions, sometimes by statutory codification. The other part, and the one we're

17. *See Kennedy v. Sheriff of E. Baton Rouge*, 935 So. 2d 669, 685 (La. 2006) ("In Louisiana, defamation is a delict governed by LSA-C.C. art. 2315 [a provision of the state's Civil Code]. Nevertheless, in examining the parameters of the tort, Louisiana courts have drawn on and borrowed from the common law terminology.").

interested in right now, is related to yet another sense in which people use the term "common law."[18]

The "common law" as a tradition of legal thought and judicial decision that is shared across distinct and autonomous jurisdictions is undoubtedly a reality. This tradition goes beyond common law as merely a preference for cases over codes, as in the common law/civil law distinction: "common law" in the sense I am now using it is not merely the absence of a code but the presence of a complex intellectual culture, a web of ideas, concepts, and predispositions that one encounters in law school and continues to learn in practice—what I earlier called the common law vision, viewed as a tradition of thought and practice. Lawyers trained in this tradition may differ wildly over particular issues, but they will almost certainly agree about far more, and even their disagreements are likely to take place within boundaries roughly defined by the disputes of the past and the resolutions that different common law courts have reached and accept in the present.

The professional culture that common lawyers share is deeper than the particular disagreements, however important, that divide them. No one makes us think and argue within this shared professional culture: we do so because this is what we have learned, beginning with the fall 1L semester, that it means to think and argue like a lawyer in the legal systems of the United States.

(7) I want to mention one more sense in which people sometimes use the term "the common law." One of the most redoubtable of modern American lawyers, Justice Antonin Scalia, described what he called "the *attitude* of the common law judge as a mind-set that asks, 'What is the most desirable resolution of this case?'" and seeks to get to that conclusion, if necessary in ways that break with existing legal understandings. Justice Scalia had serious reservations about this mind-set—he described "first-year law school," for example, as "exhilarating because it consists of playing common law judge, which in turn consists of playing king—devising out of the brilliance of one's own mind, those laws that ought to govern mankind." This was not a compliment: Scalia thought that modern American judges and lawyers are far too willing to be "cre-

18. The Uniform Law Commission and the American Law Institute are two of the chief "institutionalized means" for achieving interstate legal agreement. They are discussed in chapter three.

ative" in arriving at the answers they personally think best on political, social, economic, or moral grounds that may have little or nothing to do with the preferences of American society or the products of American democratic politics.[19]

Other American lawyers have agreed about the existence of this attitude of always looking for the best answer to a legal question, but have thought it a virtue. One of my own fall semester 1L teachers was a great constitutional lawyer named Charles L. Black, Jr. Black liked to describe law as an art. What he meant by this, in part, was that lawyers in the common law tradition are *and ought to be* trying "to shape the world," and that as a result "all good work in law is oriented toward a good result." Unlike Justice Scalia, Professor Black didn't think this makes the common law attitude an invitation to play king or queen, or to impose the brilliance of one's own insights on the rest of us—Black insisted, for example, that the lawyer as creative artist must always bring his or her thinking to the test of the "techniques [of legal argument] sanctioned as legitimate within our legal culture." But for Professor Black, unlike Justice Scalia, the common law attitude that aims at "attaining justice, or at a lower level, practicability and political, commercial or human-relations wisdom" is a good thing, not a regrettable byproduct of the 1L year and judicial hubris.[20]

It's not my objective, in this book, to decide who is right, the justice or the professor, about how to evaluate the common law as an attitude. There are strong arguments both ways, and I believe that we need not and should not choose for the purpose of learning American law. Law, law as it has been understood and practiced in American society, is neither entirely distinct from justice nor simply a tool by which judges (or so-called elite lawyers more generally) are empowered to define "justice" and "law" as they like. But you should be aware that speaking about "the common law" can be a way of participating in this important and on-going debate.

★ ★ ★

19. Scalia, *A Matter of Interpretation* 13, 7 (1997).

20. Black, *The Humane Imagination* 19, 20, 30 (1986).

I've given you seven different meanings for the term "the common law." We use the term in these different ways because of English and American historical experience, not out of logical or conceptual necessity. "The life of the law has not been logic, but experience."

Looking at American law from an historical perspective, we speak of the common law to refer to the broad tradition of substantive and procedural law that the legal systems of the American states took over after Independence from the medieval and early modern royal courts of England. We talk about the common law as an intellectual tradition and a family of jurisdictions in contrast to the civil law because for complex and partially obscure reasons medieval England did not follow the rest of Western Europe in receiving the rediscovered Roman law of Justinian as the basis of its jurisprudence. Damages are the paradigmatic common law (or legal) remedy while the injunction is equitable because historically in England they were administered by separate courts of common law and equity. We refer to "the common law" of property and torts and crimes because the royal courts asserted jurisdiction over those matters and struggled to impose a uniform national law, a law common to the entire kingdom, on these issues and so displace an original mass of divergent regional customs and procedures. We can use "the common law" to refer to the professional culture shared by twenty-first century American lawyers because their shared modes of thought and debate originated in the professional culture of the English common law bench and bar. And as for the common law as an attitude pushing American lawyers to look, creatively, for the best solution to the case—well, the disagreement between Justice Scalia and Professor Black about whether the attitude is good or bad would have looked perfectly familiar to an English lawyer around the year 1600... as we shall see below.

The varying senses in which people use the expression "the common law" are just an example of the ways in which the law, its language, concepts and institutions, are stamped by the experience of a particular history that begins a long time ago and on the other side of the Atlantic. Holmes once said that "the past gives us our vocabulary and fixes the limits of our imagination; we cannot get away from it."[21] Since that is so, I want us to turn now to that past, and see where our words and our imaginative limits originate.

---

21. Holmes, Learning and Science (1895), in *The Essential Holmes* 184.

TWO

The English Origins of American Law

Let's start in the year 1150. King Stephen is perched, precariously, on the throne of England, but the political reality is that the realm remains torn by an intermittent civil war, now over a decade old, between Stephen and his supporters and the partisans of his cousin, the Empress Matilda. Civil wars tend to be bad for legal systems, for obvious reasons, but even apart from the anarchy resulting from the conflict, England in 1150 is a legal mess. There are no centralized legal institutions at all—the king holds court, in the legal as well as regal sense, but does so wherever he happens to be. The royal court, the *curia* (or *aula*) *regis*, is a court of law in a largely ad hoc fashion involving no clear distinctions among its judicial, legislative, and executive functions. In 1150 a bewildering variety of other institutions have the resolution of legal disputes as one of their functions—manorial courts, sheriff's courts, church courts, and on and on—and all of these have their own ways of dealing with disputes. There are no professional judges, or lawyers, nor any lay juries, no trials in our sense, nor any settled means of appealing to some other institution from an unjust outcome. Methods of proof—not really the right term, perhaps—include compurgation (where someone accused of a crime swears he's innocent of an accusation and brings a set of oath helpers who swear that his oath is true) and ordeal by battle, hot iron, or water. There is a lot of substantive law, but it is entirely regional—the law of Kent in the Southeast, of Wessex in the Southwest, Mercia in the Midlands, of the Danelaw in the North—and other than the canon law of the church courts it consists almost entirely of custom. Almost nothing in the English legal world of 1150 would seem familiar to you or me.

Now skip forward to 1300, and you and I will find a vast change: the common law, in the historical sense as a set of institutions and a legal tradition, has come into being. Many features of the legal landscape would look strangely familiar. The central royal courts, which are now distinctly legal tribunals quite separate from the monarch's council or ceremonial "court," are busy creating a law common across England. Furthermore, they are attempting to impose, with remarkable and increasing success, their paramount authority over other legal decisionmakers within the kingdom. I'm not going to try to trace the chronology of these developments. The goal of this chapter is instead to point out certain features of the common law as it developed in England in the medieval and early modern eras that I believe will serve our goal of understanding the foundations of twenty-first century law in the United States.[1]

Choosing which features to present is a challenge, for there are many plausible candidates. For example, medieval English law's deep concern with the legal control of land has decisively shaped the law of real property, which you are likely to study in the first year. This is not just in the obvious impact of medieval feudalism on twenty-first century law—every reference to a landowner's title in fee simple absolute takes us straight back to the world of lords and vassals. More generally, the language and conceptual framework of the old common law of property underlies our modern ideas of legal and constitutional rights.

Or again, one might examine the ways in which the history of the early common law is reflected in contemporary American law's intense concern with the jurisdiction of federal and state courts. As suggested above, for half a millennium, English legal history was in large measure the story of the fight by the royal, common law courts to extend their jurisdiction over ever-broader areas of English life. The common law judges and lawyers waged this fight in the teeth of intermittently fierce resistance from competing legal institutions, local courts, church courts, the chancery, Parliament (as it slowly separated out from the *curia regis*), and the Crown. The mysteries of federal court jurisdiction, of subject matter v. personal jurisdiction and *Pennoyer v. Neff* (if you haven't met this famous case yet, you will![2]), and so on, reflect in ways both large and

1. See the endnote on the traditional royal courts at Westminster.

2. 95 U.S. 74 (1878) (discussing constitutional limitations on personal jurisdiction). When lawyers mention *Pennoyer* outside court documents they often add something like

small the struggles of the common law courts to impose their authority on other loci of power, including the authority to determine just what powers those other institutions might legitimately exercise.

Rather than focus on the critical role of English legal history in the evolution of specific areas of law, however, we shall look at three overall themes that reveal the deep influence of the historical experience of English law in the present-day contours of American law: insularity, proceduralism, and the idea of reason.

Insularity

As we've already seen, the common law of England did not participate in the broad culture of civil law that developed in Western Europe after the rediscovery of Justinian's Code around 1070. You could study his *Corpus Juris Civilis* in medieval England at Oxford and Cambridge, and Roman law was influential in certain non-common law tribunals. But Justinian played little role in the debates of the common lawyers, and both procedurally and substantively the common law developed in substantial isolation from law on the Continent. This had all sorts of ramifications that continue today.

Medieval Roman law was, first and foremost, an academic subject, the product as much of the eleventh- and twelfth-century universities as of the sixth-century emperor. The jurists who developed it were in close intellectual contact with the wider intellectual world: to this day, the work of academic commentators has a prestige and authority in civil law societies that it generally does not among judges and practicing lawyers in the common law world.

The medieval common law, in contrast, was the preserve of the professional lawyers, and it was not taught in the universities: you learned law through exposure to argument and debate among judges and practitioners. Unlike the continental jurists, even those common lawyers with a scholarly bent were seldom interested in or even knowledgeable about what contemporary theologians and philosophers were saying:

"that bane of first-year law students." *See, e.g.*, Ira Brad Matetsky, The Longest-Serving Justice Retires, 24 Green Bag 2d 43, 44 (2020).

the common lawyers' erudition was a guild learning, quite distinct from, and on its face hardly related to, broader intellectual currents.

An incident involving a great sixteenth-century common lawyer, Sir Thomas More, will illustrate the point. Once when More was in Flanders on a diplomatic mission, a distinguished scholar invited any comer to debate him on any question in any area of learning. More appeared and asked simply whether beasts of the plow, taken in withernam, could be replevied. The Continental scholar, needless to say, had no idea what to say about that recondite question of common law and was embarrassed into silence. More's admirers no doubt told this story as a compliment to their hero, but the scholar whom More took down a notch was not quite the fool that he might seem: he had issued his challenge while thinking in terms of an intellectual culture shared among all learned Western Europeans. More himself was a distinguished participant in the high culture of Western Europe, but he was also able to draw on a body of knowledge about which no one who was not an English lawyer knew anything.[3]

The professional and intellectual isolation of the medieval and early modern common law still shows up in all sorts of ways in American law today. Think about your own first-year classes: no matter how much economics or psychology or philosophy or political science is incorporated into your courses, the heart of the 1L experience, for the vast majority of American law students, remains the acquisition of a body of concepts and a specialized language that is unique to lawyers in the common law tradition. You may not hear again about More's puzzler,[4] but you will learn a lot about terms and concepts such as consideration in contract law and contributory negligence in tort that are just as ar-

3. *See* 3 Blackstone, *Commentaries* *149 n.(v). I am following Blackstone's canonical version of the story, the details of which varied among More's early biographers. For a somewhat different understanding of More's "wicked practical joke" and its point, *see* J. Duncan M. Derrett, Withernam: A Legal Practical Joke of Sir Thomas More, 7 Catholic Lawyer 211, 222 (1961).

4. Ah yes, and what was the correct answer to More's question? Presumably "no," although had I been there I would have prudently joined the scholar in quietly sitting down! Replevin is a proceeding that provisionally restores disputed chattels (personal property as opposed to realty) to a plaintiff pending resolution of the plaintiff's claim that the chattels have been wrongfully taken, while withernam was a (generally obsolete) writ by which chattels were lawfully seized by the sheriff pending resolution of the dispute. According to Professor Derrett, there was also an act of Parliament specifically addressing beasts of the plough. *See id.* at 214.

cane, just as limited to the guild, as the common law of More's day, and you will be taught, for the most part, by instructors whose intellectual background and training are primarily professional.[5]

Another product of the common law's insularity, and perhaps its most prominent, was the lay jury. In the rest of Western Europe, early medieval modes of popular participation in legal dispute resolution gradually disappeared: they fit uneasily in the so-called inquisitorial procedures of the civil law. In contrast, in England, the expansion into the countryside of royal law administered by professionalized royal judges led to the opposite result. From 1166 on, the royal judges relied on what we now call the grand jury in determining who should be tried for criminal violations of the king's peace; in the period after the church effectively abolished trial by ordeal in 1215, the judges came to rely on petit juries as adjudicators: speaking broadly, the judges decided questions of procedure and proof, while the jury applied the standards of the community to what the jury believed to be the facts. Don't misunderstand: there were many, many differences between a medieval English jury and a modern American one, perhaps the most important being that the medieval jurors originally acted on the basis of what they knew rather than on the basis of what other people told them, and their transformation from what we would call witnesses to the "triers of fact" of today took a long time. But the prominent role of civil and criminal juries in the United States of the twenty-first century would be inexplicable apart from its English historical background.[6]

The existence of the lay jury in turn gave rise to other unique features of the common law. Since the medieval and early modern jury had almost unlimited discretion in how to decide the cases submitted to it, from an early point the common law judges sought ways to control which cases got to the jury and what sorts of evidence the jurors could consider. Almost the entirety of the law of evidence, as well as many

5. The number of law professors with a Ph.D. (the union card of twenty-first century university teachers) is steadily increasing, but my sense is that the impact of that fact remains least evident in first-year teaching.

6. With respect to the jury as in certain other respects, the legal systems of the United States preserve features of the common law that have withered in other jurisdictions in the common-law tradition: civil juries have almost entirely disappeared in England and Wales, for example. Ironically, in many contemporary civil-law countries, juries made up in part or whole of non-lawyers are used in certain types of cases.

aspects of civil procedure, thus find their origins in the effort of medieval judges to set limits to what medieval juries could do in the only way the judges could. The jury system, itself a result of English law's insularity, thus points us to the second aspect of the English experience I want to underline: English law's proceduralism.

A Focus on Procedure

In the medieval common law, what lawyers and judges mostly argued over was procedure. In civil cases, the arguments revolved around the fact that in order to commence a civil action in a royal court the plaintiff needed to purchase a document called a writ from the king's Chancery that directed the sheriff to require the defendant to do right or alternatively to appear in court. Originally the Chancery issued writs using whatever language seemed appropriate, but over time the writs' language became formulaic and after about 1275 the Chancery ceased to devise new writs at all: the plaintiff had to fit his case within one of the "forms of action" allowed by an existing writ or fail to get the case before a common law court. For centuries, common lawyers spent much of their time arguing about the proper use of the writs and the defensive pleadings available in this or that form of action. It would be a mistake to see these medieval lawyers as mindless formalists worrying over magic formulas: beneath the procedural surface issues of substantive justice often can clearly be seen. But the legal debate, and much of the lawyers' thinking, was organized in terms of the forms of action—which writ should be used—rather than by rules of substantive law, as we might expect. The great legal historian Henry Maine famously wrote, the "substantive law was at first... secreted in the interstices of procedure; and the early lawyer can only see the law through the envelope of its technical forms."[7]

Let's look at an actual example: *Waldon v. Mareschal* (1369).[8] William Waldon's horse was sick, and he made a deal with John to treat the horse. ("Marshal," by the way, wasn't John's last name but his profession—he was a horse veterinarian.) When the horse died, William obtained a writ

7. Henry S. Maine, *Dissertations on Early Law and Custom* 389 (1883).

8. Y.B. Mich. 43 Edw. III (C.P. 1369), in J.H. Baker & S.F.C. Milsom, *Sources of English Legal History: Private Law to 1750* 359–60 (1986).

of trespass from the Chancery to try his claim against John in the Court of Common Pleas. William's factual claim was that John was careless in treating the horse, and John's defense was that he was not, but the debate recorded in the yearbook[9] is almost entirely about which writ William should have used.

After some initial skirmishing over whether William's writ had the words "against the king's peace" in it (it didn't), and whether that mattered, the main argument began with Dr. John's lawyer telling the court, "William's claim is that my client promised to cure the horse but didn't. But when you're complaining about a broken promise you need to use the writ of covenant. William is here with a writ of trespass—so he should be thrown out of court before getting to the jury."

This is an excellent example of a perfectly sound medieval common law argument, but William's lawyer had an answer. "We aren't complaining about a broken promise, we're complaining about our claim that Dr. John made William's horse die. That is the sort of wrong that you *do* use a writ of trespass for: in fact there is no other writ that we can use to get into royal court."

Dr. John's lawyer wasn't done, though. This time his argument went like this: "William's claim is that my client killed the horse, and that means he needed to use a writ of trespass saying that Dr. John acted 'with force and arms.' But his writ doesn't say that... so William should be thrown out of court."

Unfortunately for Dr. John, William's lawyer once again had an answer. "We don't say that Dr. John killed the horse but that he let the horse die by his carelessness, so the writ of trespass we've got is the right one." End of discussion.

---

9. The yearbooks were in essence reports, written in the "law French" used in the medieval English common law system, of the arguments that lawyers and judges made in court. Unlike modern law reports, their purpose was not to state controlling precedents and rules of law; they were, instead, "designed to teach the techniques of legal argument... the way to persuade a judge." The reporters, who remained anonymous, "must have been in court [and] must have been legally sophisticated," and although apparently stenographic, they "summarize[ed] rather than portray[ed] the arguments." Thomas Lund, *The Creation of the Common Law* 1–3 & n. 7 (2015). Professor Lund's book is a wonderful introduction to and window on the common law in the enormously creative era of William de Bereford, chief justice of the Court of Common Pleas from 1309 to 1326.

The first thing to note is that we don't know from the yearbook who won *Waldon v. Mareschal*—the yearbook doesn't record what the jury's verdict was. The account of the case ends with the lawyers stating that they are ready to have the jury decide whether Dr. John acted carelessly or not as a matter of fact, but the yearbook writer wasn't really interested in what the jury decided was the truth of the matter in William's case against John. What was important, to the writer and (we may confidently assume) to the legal profession as a whole, was the debate over what writ the plaintiff ought to use in this sort of situation. In this instance we happen to know that the plaintiff's lawyer persuaded the judges that the plaintiff should get a trial but often enough the yearbooks don't even tell us that: instead, they simply record whatever parts of the debate among the lawyers and judges the yearbook scribe thought useful or interesting.[10]

It would be easy to make fun of the lawyers and judges in *Waldon v. Mareschal* and the legal tradition they exemplify. Talk about technicalities: whether William gets a shot at royal justice depends in part on just which words the Chancery clerk included in the writ. Non-lawyers have little patience with these sorts of "legalistic" quibbles, and one sees their point. But I also want us to note that there is substance lurking behind the argument over which writ William should use. Right underneath the surface of their disputes over words like covenant and "by force and arms" lay serious questions of substantive justice and social organization. If William's writ of trespass won't get him into royal court, then the king's justice does not extend to situations involving alleged negligence on the part of a horse doctor, and perhaps other healers as well: as his lawyer says, "we can have no other writ." But Dr. John's lawyer had a point as well: if justice is to be done, we ought to be clear about what William claims was John's legal wrongdoing: was it a breach of promise, or a deliberate, destructive act, or negligence in carrying out his trade? The substantive implication of the court's decision that William was using the right writ was that royal justice was concerned not just with deliberate injuries but with careless behavior as well. As Maine said, the

10. "Modern litigants [or really their lawyers] refer to court reports to establish their rights; no one referred to the medieval [yearbook] reports to establish rights." Occasionally someone in a yearbook discussion would refer to the court's "official records, the 'plea rolls.'" *Id.* at 1 & n. 3 (bracketed words are my additions).

substance of the early common law may be hidden away in procedural corners, but it's already there.

The English common law's proceduralism, and in particular the role of the forms of action, has cast a long shadow over contemporary American law. Once again, think about the first-year curriculum. Why do you study landlord/tenant law (surely an example of a relationship based on a deal) in your property class, while you learn about restitution (a remedy for the unjust enrichment of one person laying claim to property values that ought to belong to another) in contracts? Answer: largely forgotten procedural rules. The same historical background explains much that goes on in the practice of American law. Little as our modern rules of pleading and procedure resemble those of 1369, we still rely on procedure to define legal claims, channel legal arguments, and serve the social good of resolving disputes according to shared, public norms. A twenty-first century plaintiff will almost certainly not have his claim tossed out of court because someone entered the wrong words on his complaint, but what a twenty-first century William must prove to recover damages from his horse's veterinarian, and how those damages will be measured if he prevails, probably will depend on whether his claim and proof are structured by the concept of negligence (a tort) or warranty (a contract), a distinction that stems from the lines the common law courts drew among the old forms of action. A great legal scholar once wrote that "we have buried" the "forms of action... but still they rule us from their graves."[11] He was right.

The Law as Reason

Sometime in the 1220s or 30s, a common lawyer and ecclesiastic—probably William de Raley, who was a royal judge and later a bishop—composed a very substantial treatise in Latin on *The Laws and Customs of England*; sometime later the book was edited and updated by Raley's pupil, Henry de Bracton, and the book usually goes by his name. *Bracton* quickly became obsolescent on many specific issues, but in one critical respect it anticipated the path of the future: the book very clearly distinguished the authority of the law, which rests on reason, from forms

11. Frederic W. Maitland, *The Forms of Action at Common Law* 2 (1909).

of political authority that stem from the will of those in power. Indeed, *Bracton* asserted that "law makes the king... for there is no king where the will rules rather than the law." This was a remarkable inversion of the old Roman law dictum that "the will of the prince has the force of law." Furthermore, *Bracton* hints—and later common lawyers would trumpet the claim—that the law, as it is understood within the professional guild of lawyers, is to be equated with reason itself, and as a consequence is the measure of political authority.[12]

Consider the case of *Flaundres v. Rycheman*, which came before the Court of Common Pleas in 1344.[13] In the course of a procedural discussion—what else?!—the plaintiff's lawyer, Robert Thorpe, cited earlier cases supporting his client's position. The first time Thorpe did so, his argument was brushed aside by one of the judges, who denied that old cases, even those in which famous judges participated, ought to be controlling: "One has heard speak of that which Bereford and Herle did in such a case... but nevertheless, no precedent is of such force as reason." Undaunted, Thorpe tried again, pointing out to the judges, quite reasonably, that the principle of treating similar cases similarly is essential to a well-functioning legal system, one that can guide people's conduct and resolve controversies fairly. The following exchange took place:

> *Thorpe*: I think you will do as others have done in the same case, or else we do not know what the law is.
> HILLARY J: It is the will of the Justices.
> STONORE CJ: No; law is reason.

You can find most of our contemporary debates over jurisprudence and constitutional theory in this little dialogue: both lawyer Thorpe's insistence that the demands of stability and fairness call for adherence to

---

12. 2 Henry de Bracton, *De Legibus et Consuetudinibus Angliae (On the Laws and Customs of England)* 33 (George E. Woodbine ed. & Samuel E. Thorne trans. 1968). This formulation of the Roman law principle originated with the great third-century C.E. jurist Ulpian, who may not have meant it to be quite the uncompromising statement of autocratic authority it later came to stand for. The modern English translation of Justinian's *Digest* edited by Alan Watson translates Ulpian's Latin (*Quod principi placuit, legis habet vigorem*) as "A decision given by the emperor has the force of a statute." 1 *The Digest of Justinian* 1.1.4.1, at 14 (Alan Watson rev. ed. 1998).

13. *Flaundres v. Rycheman* (C.P. 1344), *Year Books of Edward III, 1344*, 377 (Luke O. Pike ed. 1905). Bereford (see note 9 above) and William Herle were prominent Common Pleas judges earlier in the fourteenth century.

precedent and Justice Roger Hillary's retort that the law itself is an assertion of political will have their present-day adherents. But it is Chief Justice John Stonore's echo of *Bracton* that is of present interest. No, Stonore insisted, the law is neither blind adherence to tradition and precedent nor the exercise of raw power: law, at least the common law, is reason, and by implication the exercise of power, whether by judges, other officials, or private persons, is to be measured and limited by the reason of the law.

A central figure in this and other aspects of English legal history is Sir Edward Coke.[14] Lord Coke (as he was generally known afterwards) served briefly as a rather ferocious attorney general for Queen Elizabeth I, and then as chief justice of Common Pleas and then King's Bench under King James I, until James, worn out by Coke's stubborn refusal to accommodate the king's views, fired him in 1616. (Royal judges in this era served at the pleasure of the monarch, and by 1616 King James was most displeased with Coke.) After Coke's death in 1634 he became a semi-legendary figure in the collective memory of the legal profession, a process that Coke's many legal writings helped to promote. Coke emphatically agreed with Chief Justice Stonore that the law is reason and stressed a further point that Stonore had left implicit: it is the law as understood within the common law tradition and by the profession which is the reason that should govern public affairs. "For reason is the life of the Law, nay the common Law it selfe is nothing else but reason, which is to be understood of an artificiall perfection of reason, gotten by long study, observation, and experience, and not of every mans naturall reason." It is this "legall reason," embodied in the "customs and courses of...the king's courts," that is supreme in "the government of this Realme."[15]

It was Coke's good fortune, though it probably didn't seem that way at the time, to sit as a judge during the reign of James I (1603–25). James

---

14. The standard modern pronunciation of Lord Coke's name is "cook," as in the person who makes the food. An anecdote about Coke confirms that his name and the common noun sounded the same. Apparently Cook and his contemporaries pronounced both name and noun more like "kook," which carries the wrong connotation today.

15. Coke, *The First Part of the Institutes of the Laws of England* 97b (1608) in 2 *The Selected Writings of Sir Edward Coke* 701 (Steve Sheppard ed. 2003). The language about "customs and courses" is from a case Coke reported. *See Lane's Case*, 2 Co. Rep. 16b (C.P. 1596).

was a Scot, brought up in the predominantly Roman-law culture of that kingdom, of which he was sovereign from 1567 (at age one), and a firm believer in the God-given prerogatives of the king. What to Coke was obvious and long-standing common law thinking appeared to James as the monstrous claim by the king's own judicial agents to dictate to the monarch from whom they derived all their authority. The idea that the law as declared by the common law courts measures both individual liberties and governmental authority was forged in large measure in Coke's conflicts with James.

The most dramatic confrontation between the two took place rather early on in their stormy relationship. The occasion was a dispute between Chief Justice Coke's Court of Common Pleas and an ecclesiastical High Commission, headed by the Archbishop of Canterbury and deriving its authority directly from the king. In 1607 and 1608, Coke's court repeatedly issued writs of prohibition forbidding the church tribunal from exercising jurisdiction over secular matters or arresting lay persons; the Archbishop in return denied the legal authority of the common law courts to interfere with the High Commission. Unable to persuade either the judges or the ecclesiastics to back down, King James convened a meeting of all concerned in November 1608 at which he announced that he himself would decide the legal question in dispute. The Archbishop agreed that the king, the fount of justice in England, was "by the Word of God" fully entitled to "take what cases he shall please... and may determine them himself." Coke's response was in the tradition of his predecessor Stonore, but not calculated to please James.

> The king in his own person cannot adjudge any case... [legal disputes] ought to be determined and adjudged in some Court of Justice, according to the Law and Custom of England.

James, perhaps trying to be conciliatory, remarked that he agreed that "the Law was founded upon reason, but that he thought he and others had reason as well as the judges."

> To which it was answered by me, that true it was, that God had endowed his Majesty with excellent science, great endowments of nature; but his Majesty was not learned in the Lawes of his Realm of England, and causes which concern the life, or inheritance, or goods, or fortunes of his Subjects... are not to

> be decided by naturall reason but by the artificiall reason and judgment of the Law.... And that the Law was the Golden metwand and measure to try the Causes of the Subjects; and which protected his Majesty in safety and peace: With which the King was greatly offended, and said, that then he should be under the Law, which was treason to affirm.... To which I said, that Bracton saith *Quod Rex non debet esse sub homine, sed sub Deo et Lege* [The king ought not to be under any man, but under God and the Law].[16]

At some point in the ensuing hullabaloo James started to pummel Coke, who fell to his knees and begged the king's pardon "if His Majesty thought he had gone beyond his duty and allegiance." The concession, however, was tactical and temporary. As Coke's biographer put it,

> It was that or a cell in the Tower. The Chief Justice knelt, and rose, and went out into November city streets.... Next morning, a new prohibition, under Coke's seal, went out to High Commission from the Court of Common Pleas.[17]

Anglo-American lawyers have a long-standing habit of telling themselves self-congratulatory stories, and it would be a mistake to think that the only good arguments in this confrontation between king and judge were on the lawyer's side. James, who was no fool, pointed out that the logic of Coke's position would free the common lawyers and their guild learning, and above all the judges of the common law courts, from responsibility to anyone but themselves: "If the judges interpret the laws themselves and suffer no one else to interpret, they may easily make, of the laws, shipmen's hose," formless socks that the courts can shape as they wish.[18]

James's accusation remains as apposite today as it was in 1608. Contemporary American lawyers and politicians argue incessantly over

---

16. *Prohibitions del Roy*, 12 Co. Rep. 63–65 (1607) in 1 *Selected Writings* 479–81.

17. Catherine Drinker Bowen, *The Lion and the Throne: The Life and Times of Sir Edward Coke* 306 (1957). Bowen's biography is old, and it was popular rather than scholarly writing when it was new, but it vividly presents the Coke of legal memory and myth, who is the Coke that matters for understanding American law.

18. Roland G. Usher, *James I and Sir Edward Coke*, 18 Eng. Hist. Rev. 664, 669 (1903) (quoting James I as related in Sir Julius Caesar's *Notes Touching Prohibitions*).

whether this or that judicial decision is a faithful application of the law or "legislation from the bench," and many academic observers think that Coke's "artificial reason" is what James thought, professional smoke and mirrors behind which judges and lawyers pursue their own policy preferences. Who is right on these great matters I shall not try to resolve here, although an important aspect of the next three years is the preparation your legal training should give you to come to your own conclusions. Whatever you decide, I believe there is no doubt that contemporary American law is shaped, through and through, by the claim of English common lawyers such as Coke that the law is or should be reason itself, and that in our legal system the reason which governs legal affairs is to be sought by employing the tools of thought and argument of the legal profession.

"The life of the law has not been logic: it has been experience." As I have tried to indicate, it is clear that in a multitude of ways, Holmes was right about that, and equally right when he claimed that we cannot escape the past. But perhaps you recall that I also quoted him to the effect that the value of understanding our historical experience lies, at least in part, in freeing us from the dead hand of the past: Holmes, you will recall, wanted us to acquire his own "enlightened skepticism" about "the worth" of that experience as it lives on in the forms of the law.[19] Chief Justice Coke believed deeply in the social value of what I've called the common law mindset, but Justice Scalia would beg to differ. We should not accept uncritically the value or wisdom of our legal tradition's experience. After all, neither insularity nor an obsession with procedure nor the equation of professional jargon with reason itself is self-evidently a good thing. In the end, you may conclude that what this history does is suggest the need for a more thorough legal updating than we have as yet undertaken: more twenty-first century logic and less common law experience.

I've no doubt that is true sometimes, but I want to close this chapter by pointing to an aspect of the English legal experience that is, I think, of inestimable value in contemporary American law. It's easy to see the ways in which the old common lawyers' robust belief in the value of their guild traditions was often driven by collective self-interest even if they genuinely believed their self-aggrandizing claim to be defending the law

19. Holmes, The Path of the Law (1897), in *The Essential Holmes* 170.

as the perfection of reason in human affairs. But that isn't the entire lesson to be learned from the English experience. Over time, and for complex historical reasons, the self-interested insistence of the common lawyers that the law—their law—is (as Coke told King James) "the Golden metwand and measure" of power, came to play a role in English life that transcended the selfish interests of the profession or of the ruling classes that the lawyers generally served.[20]

The most memorable description to me of what this last statement means is found in a book called *Whigs and Hunters*, written by the great English historian E.P. Thompson. Thompson's book is an examination of the origins and enforcement of a 1723 act of Parliament usually known as the Black Act, which introduced the death penalty for an array of heinous offenses such as stalking deer at night in disguise, damaging fish ponds, and cutting down trees in gardens. The Black Act was as pure an example of class legislation as one might fear to find: its point was to safeguard, brutally, the exclusive claim of the aristocracy to a wide range of natural resources. As Thompson put it,

> I have shown in this study a political oligarchy inventing callous and oppressive laws to serve its own interests. I have shown judges who ... were subject to political influence, whose sense of justice was humbug, and whose interpretation of the laws served only to enlarge their inherent class bias. Indeed, I think that this study has shown that for many of England's governing elite the rules of law were a nuisance, to be manipulated and bent in what ways they could.[21]

None of this surprised Thompson, an historian of strong left-wing political views who expected all along to find that the Black Act was a means for oppressing the lower classes. But to his surprise, he found something else as well.

The common law judges and barristers on whom it fell to administer the Black Act may have been toadies and tools of the aristocracy, but they were also the heirs of *Bracton* and Stonore and Coke. They were (mostly) quite ready to employ the act to grind the faces of the poor, but they insisted (mostly) that the forms and procedures of the common law

20. *See Prohibitions del Roy*, 12 Co. Rep. at 63–65.

21. Thompson, *Whigs and Hunters: The Origin of the Black Act* 265 (1975).

tradition had to be observed when doing so, with the result that sometimes the act failed of its oppressive purpose, sometimes "the Government itself retired from the courts defeated," sometimes the lawyers' obsession with procedures meant that the powerful could not work their will on some powerless individual.[22]

Thompson found himself, apparently much to his surprise, driven to a final, and less despairing conclusion. The allegiance of England's political leadership "to the rhetoric of law was largely humbug. But I do not conclude from this that the rule of law itself was humbug."

> The rhetoric and the rules of a society are something a great deal more than sham.... They may disguise the true realities of power, but at the same time, they may curb that power and check its intrusions.... I am not starry eyed about this at all.... But the rule of law itself, the imposing of effective inhibitions upon power and the defence of the citizen from power's all-intrusive claim, seems to me to be an unqualified human good. To deny or belittle this good is... a desperate error of intellectual abstraction.... It is to throw away a whole inheritance of struggle *about* law, whose continuity can never be fractured without bringing men and women into immediate danger.[23]

The extent to which law in the twenty-first century United States suffers from inequities or hypocrisies parallel to those that Thompson identified in the eighteenth-century Black Act is debatable and debated: certainly there is no consensus on that question. But I agree, with Thompson, that the rule of law as an effective inhibition on power, and its sociological rooting in a tradition (however self-serving) of lawyers and judges insisting on the forms of law, is an unqualified human good. Law in the United States owes this good, to the extent we possess it, in large measure to the experience left to us by the history of English law.

---

22. *Id.*

23. *Id.* at 265–66.

THREE

The Creation of American Law, or Making It up as We Go Along

In 1799, the New Jersey legislature enacted a most interesting law. The statute made it unlawful for any litigant or judge to cite any English case decided later than July 4, 1776, or "any compilation, commentary, digest, lecture, treatise or other explanation or exposition of the common law" whatever. King George III had recognized American independence over fifteen years earlier, but it would seem that anti-English feelings had not disappeared. Nor was this sort of legal Anglophobia limited to the State House in Trenton: English law was the object of recurrent criticism throughout much of the early nineteenth century.

To see why, let's look at the case of Robert Rantoul. Rantoul's name is hardly a household word in the twenty-first century, but for the twenty years up to his premature death in 1852, Rantoul was a well-known lawyer and public figure not only in his native Massachusetts but throughout the country. Rantoul was arguably the first great public interest lawyer in American history: among his causes were opposition to the Fugitive Slave Act, the right of labor to organize, the expansion of educational opportunities for the poor, and the abolition of the death penalty. Rantoul also had strong views about the English background to American law. You will recall that Lord Coke called the common law "the perfection of reason." Rantoul put his own spin on that proud claim. As he phrased it in 1836:

> The common law has been called the perfection of human reason. [It is] . . . just as alcohol is the perfection of sugar. The sub-

> tle spirit of the Common Law is reason double distilled, till what was wholesome and nutritive becomes rank poison. Reason is sweet and pleasant to the unsophisticated intellect, but this sublimated perversion of reason bewilders and perplexes and plunges its victims into mazes of error.

Rantoul had three related but distinct objections to the common law. First, since it is declared by judges, the common law is a usurpation of the role of the democratic process in republican America, and as such it is an unwelcome holdover from the aristocratic principles of England. Second, common law rules emerge in the very cases that announce and apply them instead of being enacted by the legislature in advance. "No man can tell what the common law is; therefore it is not law: for the law is a rule of action; but a rule which is unknown can govern no man's conduct.... Judge-made law is ex post facto law, and therefore unjust." Third, the means by which lawyers and judges purport to debate and decide cases at common law are an intellectual fraud: "The judge makes law, by extorting from precedents something which they do not contain. He extends his precedents, which were themselves the extension of others" and so builds up an entire system of law.[1]

As a factual matter, each of Rantoul's charges is accurate. A number of years ago, Justice Sandra Day O'Connor cheerfully acknowledged, speaking specifically about the US Supreme Court, that "of course we make law as we go along."[2] That was Rantoul's point as well, although he was talking about American courts generally and he wasn't happy about it: in a common law world, the courts make it up as they go along.[3] Rantoul had a simple solution for all this: the legislature should codify the law and enact it, which at one and the same time would make the law democratic, just and clear. As you already know, Rantoul failed, although the codification movement that he was instrumental in beginning eventually achieved some partial successes, particularly in the area of civil

1. Robert Rantoul, *Oration at Scituate* (1836) in *The Legal Mind in America* 223–24 (Perry Miller ed. 1962).

2. Jeffrey Toobin, *The Nine: Inside the Secret World of the Supreme Court* 97 (2007).

3. I recognize that Justice O'Connor might very reasonably object that there is a difference between "making law" and "making law *up* as we go along." For present purposes, however, the difference is irrelevant. Rantoul's criticism rested on the premise that judges *interpret* or *apply* law and aren't supposed to create, to *make* it. Where judges derive the law they illegitimately make (up) was for Rantoul a secondary matter.

procedure. But why did he fail? In part, the answer lay in the familiarity and adaptability of English common law both as a system of law and as an approach to legal decision: these attractions proved, in the end, too compelling to allow for its wholesale repudiation.

The American turn to English law was aided by the fact that the term "common law" was already on its way to acquiring the ambiguity and multi-faceted meaning that it possesses today. When New Jersey's legislators thought about the common law, they, like Rantoul, seem to have had in mind a legal antique full of feudal ideas and anti-democratic procedures, but for most Americans—or at least most American lawyers!—reference to the common law evoked a gauzy semi-mythical history of the struggle of liberty against power: the rights of Englishmen v. Stuart oppression, Sir Edward Coke standing up to King James I. No one in the founding era could object to Lord Coke, but once you admitted the possible existence of great good in the English legal tradition, where did you draw the line?

Another major reason that borrowing large amounts of English law was more or less inescapable was the lack of any obvious alternative. Few Americans in the founding era knew much about the complex European systems of Roman-based civil law, and the rationalized and accessible Napoleonic Code did not appear until the American politico-legal experiment had been up and running for a generation. The colonial period produced no American legal treatises to speak of, and no published judicial reports, and to learn their trade colonial era lawyers read Coke and, at the very end Blackstone, whose comprehensive treatise on English law appeared on the eve of the Revolution; after Independence American lawyers continued to do the same. Most Americans thought of the Revolution itself in remarkably legalistic ways—no taxation without representation was not just a slogan but a legal argument about the limits of Parliament's authority. The written constitutions in which the Revolutionaries attempted to codify the new political order were a political innovation of sorts, but they employed the language and concepts of English law, and the judicial decisions that began appearing in the first American law reports published in the last years of the eighteenth century show little sign that Anglophobia of the New Jersey kind had much purchase on practicing lawyers or sitting judges.

When the distinguished Virginia judge and William & Mary law professor St. George Tucker wanted to provide a comprehensive text for

American lawyers in the first years of Thomas Jefferson's administration, he did so by publishing an edition of Blackstone's *Commentaries on the Laws of England.* President Jefferson was a harsh critic of Blackstone, whom Jefferson thought a royalist toady, and Tucker was a strong political and intellectual ally of Jefferson, so it is unsurprising that "Tucker's Blackstone" was loaded with footnotes and appendices criticizing the anachronisms and inegalitarianism of English law. Nevertheless, most of the words were still Blackstone's, and Tucker's (legal) bestseller served only to increase the visibility and influence of English law. Despite the efforts of Rantoul and other critics, the future of American law would be deeply rooted in the English past.

This does not mean, of course, that American courts simply deduced how English legal principles would apply to American legal problems. The life of the law has not been logic but experience. The antebellum (pre-Civil War) bench and bar borrowed the forms of English law almost in their entirety...and then used those forms as the vehicle by which lawyers could develop a law of contract, tort, property, and so on that was markedly novel in substance. (Quick aside: Confronted with the new world of an industrializing Britain, English lawyers were doing the same thing on their side of the Atlantic, and the lines of influence went both ways.) I suggested above that it was not only the familiarity of English law but its adaptability that facilitated its adoption in this country. In one sense, to be sure, English law in the late eighteenth century had the appearance of great rigidity. Common law forms of action that on the surface had scarcely changed for centuries shaped what parties had to plead and to prove. Cases brought in the courts of equity were by this point as caught up in their own tradition-ridden processes. But here the intense proceduralism of English law made it of practical value to lawyers in the United States. The rigidity of common law and equity was procedural, formal, linguistic; its largely implicit substance was fluid and changeable. There was an inexhaustible supply of English case law demonstrating the ways by which clever lawyers and determined judges could adapt inherited forms to address novel issues and reach substantive conclusions never dreamt of by Stonore or Coke. Almost at once, American lawyers grasped the opportunities this provided for adapting law that originated in medieval Westminster or Lancaster to the needs of nineteenth-century Philadelphia and Richmond. The subterranean substance of the law could be dramatically changed while carefully preserving the familiar forms. Let us see how and why that was done.

The Development of American Law, ca. 1800 to ca. 1850

James Kent was one of the towering figures of early American law. For almost two decades Kent was a trial judge who also sat on appellate cases in his native New York. In 1814 he became that state's chief equity judge, and as "Chancellor Kent" he developed an international reputation as a jurist. After his retirement from office in 1823 Kent wrote a four-volume treatise entitled *Commentaries on American Law*; the book went through six editions in the next two decades, and continued to be updated far longer. (Holmes was the reviser of the twelfth edition, which appeared in 1873.) Kent's *Commentaries* obviously took a giant step beyond Tucker's publication of Blackstone with notes, but on its face the *Commentaries* looked like a very conservative transplantation of English law into this country. Something similar can be said about the nine weighty treatises Justice Joseph Story wrote in the 1830s and 40s in his spare time between sitting on the US Supreme Court and on circuit and giving lectures at Harvard: the erudite Story was familiar with civil and international law beyond the more parochial Kent's interests, but Story too strove to present his learning in general as a recurrence to settled ideas. Beneath the surface, however, a lot more was going on.

As it happens, we have a confidential letter that Kent wrote about his approach to judicial decisionmaking. He was specifically responding to a question about his decisions as Chancellor in the New York equity court, but he spoke for several generations of American lawyers and judges who were in fact transforming both equity and the common law.

> I took the court as if it had been a new institution, and never before known in the United States. I had nothing to guide me, and was left at liberty to assume all such... powers and jurisdiction as I thought applicable.... This gave me grand scope.... My practice was, first, to make myself perfectly and accurately master of the facts.... I saw where justice lay, and moral sense decided the court half the time; and then I sat down to search the authorities until I had examined my books. I might once in while be embarrassed by a technical rule, but I most always found principles suited to my views of the case.[4]

4. Kent, Letter to Thomas Washington (1828) in William Kent, *Memoirs and Letters of James Kent* 158–59 (1898).

Kent was no doubt more self-conscious, and at least in this private letter more candid, than most of his contemporaries, but his letter captures almost perfectly the intellectual atmosphere of American law in the first half of the 1800s: an expansive sense of freedom to shape the law to the needs of society and of justice; a deep confidence that the authorities and the books and the technical rules of English law were a resource for this shaping rather than an impediment to it; and a robust belief in the role of the courts in making law. Chancellor Kent's private confession of the "grand scope" of his judicial power in equity was Robert Rantoul's nightmare—judges invoking "the common law" as the excuse for what Rantoul thought the judges' unjust and undemocratic imposition of their will on the rest of us. And yet rather than inciting a second Revolution, by and large the work of Kent and his colleagues was widely popular. How could this be so?

Part of the answer was political, and reflects the partial success of the democratic ideals for which Rantoul was a spokesman: the profession of law itself was democratized. Requirements for admission to legal practice were loosened and the popular election of judges gradually spread, from frontier states eastward and from a means of filling local magistrates' courts to the selection of the highest judges in a state. The year before the long-retired Chancellor Kent died in 1847, New York adopted general judicial elections, and by the Civil War two thirds of the states had followed suit. The popular election of state judges remains a widespread feature of the United States legal system: in most states contestable popular elections are used to choose some or all of the state's judges.[5] As Rantoul was quick to point out, this hardly solved the other problems he saw with judge-made law, but it was more difficult to criticize the judges for being anti-democratic when they were chosen by the most democratic of means.

In explaining why pre-Civil War judges enjoyed such a free hand, however, it seems likely that a more important factor was their perceived

---

5. The National Center for State Courts answers the question of how many states elect judges in this way: "With more than 25 different selection systems, the question of which states elect judges does not have an easy answer." https://www.ncsc.org/information-and-resources/trending-topics/trending-topics-landing-pg/how-many-states-elect-judges-its-complicated! If you are interested, check out the Center's excellent data visualization webpages: https://www.ncsc.org/consulting-and-research/areas-of-expertise/court-leadership/judicial-selection.

success in the molding the substance of the law to meet the changing needs of society. Writing in the 1760s and early 1770s, Blackstone had painted a picture of English law still rooted in a largely static, rural and pre-industrial society: the legal issues that mattered were far more likely to concern land ownership than commercial credit or the relationship between manufacturers and their employees. For example, Blackstone spent little time on the law governing commercial relationships in the *Commentaries*: his main discussion of the law of contract takes up about four pages out of his four volumes. There simply wasn't much substantive contract law to discuss.

American society on the eve of Chancellor Kent's retirement was still primarily rural, but in other respects it was radically different from Blackstone's England.

> By the 1820s the process of industrialization [in the US] was far advanced. The profound shock of technological change was already being experienced, as the eighteenth century world of stagecoaches and cottage manufacture was metamorphosed into the new and unsettling world of railroads and factories.[6]

This new commercialized and industrializing society was one in which four pages on contract law was simply not enough. The substantive ambiguities of our inherited English legal forms provided the space within which Kent and his colleagues were free to devise legal rules and principles that could best accommodate the needs of commerce and industry (at least as they perceived those needs) without appearing to change the law... and even if Robert Rantoul saw through the façade and disliked what he saw, many other Americans seem to have been largely happy with the results.

This is the era in which, here and in England, many of the legal concepts and doctrines you study in your first-year classes are first given their modern substantive content. Blackstone's four pages on contracts became over 400 pages in William W. Story's 1844 American treatise, and the outline of a coherent body of tort law, centered on the concept of negligence, emerged from the grab bag of writs of *de bonis asportatis* and *quare clausum fregit* that Blackstone knew. The judges were making up, as they went along, an overtly substantive system of law ("the com-

6. Grant Gilmore & Philip Bobbitt, *The Ages of American Law* 22 (2d ed. 2014).

mon law" in the fifth meaning I gave you in chapter one), no longer wedded to the old procedural forms of action, which having played their part in the process had thereby rendered themselves obsolete.

By definition, substantive law cannot be "value-neutral," and the new law that the antebellum judges and advocates were creating generally had a definite political and moral tilt: it reflected and often seems deliberately designed to further values favored by the commercial and manufacturing classes over those embraced by agricultural producers and industrial workers, or women, or marginalized minorities. This tilt shows up across all the major substantive areas of law; I will take contract law as an example. During this period, liability for breach of contract narrowed. There is considerable evidence indicating that an English or American jury of, say, 1800, returned its verdict in a case involving the breach of a promise in accordance with the jurors' sense about who was in the right morally and without much worry over confining the damages they awarded to injury defined by the terms of a bargain; there was an expression, "smart money," for the extra damages an offended jury sometimes imposed on a defendant whom the jurors believed had behaved poorly—the additional shillings were to give him pain. This sort of free-form jury justice was unpopular with the rising business classes, who generally preferred certainty about business risks, and were leery of jurors deciding for themselves if a deal was or was not fair.

Soon after 1800, American courts began to narrow the jury's discretion in cases involving promises in a variety of ways. As early as 1804, New York adopted a stringent version of *caveat emptor*, let the buyer beware, in a case decided on appeal by a court including James Kent, who explained that the rule of *caveat emptor* satisfied "the claims of convenience" and accorded with prudent business practice and efficiency.[7] It is easy enough, I think, to imagine how such a strict rule generally benefitted the experienced and business savvy over the naive and the amateur. As the mid-century mark approached, the older view of promises as moral obligations that a jury should evaluate as such was on the verge of disappearing in the face of this business-oriented understanding of contract law: a contract, the cases increasingly insisted, is an arms-length deal negotiated without deceit but also without generosity by coldly self-interested parties.

7. *Seixas v. Woods*, 2 Cai. R. 48, 55–56 (N.Y. 1804) (opinion of Kent, J.).

One means the courts developed for preventing juries from following the older, moral obligation view, involved reworking the idea of "consideration." In the older English common law, consideration was basically a pleading requirement, but in the early nineteenth century it became a device for distinguishing "contracts" on the commercial model from gratuitous promises. The 1845 Alabama case of *Kirksey v. Kirksey*, often included in 1L casebooks today, will serve as an example. The plaintiff was the defendant's sister-in-law, but lived some distance away. On learning of his brother's death, the defendant wrote her a letter offering her "a place to raise your family: . . . I have more open land than I can tend; and on the account of your situation, and that of your family, I feel like I want you and the children to do well." Soon after getting her brother-in-law's letter, the plaintiff simply abandoned her farm and undertook the long trip with her children. In doing so she ignored another part of the defendant's letter, in which he advised her to get secure title to her farm and sell it before undertaking any move. The relationship evidently soured: after two years in what the Alabama Reports describe as "comfortable houses [with] land to cultivate, [the defendant] notified her to remove, and put her in a house, not comfortable, in the woods, which he afterwards required her to leave." The jury returned a verdict for the plaintiff of two hundred dollars, and her brother-in-law appealed.[8]

Half a century earlier, the argument before the appellate court would likely have been directed toward the possible mismatch between the plaintiff's pleading and her proof, and she would probably have kept her verdict, which was quite large for the time and place and almost certainly shows that the jurors thought the brother-in-law had behaved badly. But then a verdict for him would probably have been upheld as well, since it would have been equally within the province of the jury to decide that she had acted foolishly in not taking his advice about selling her farm. By 1845, however, the argument was over the substance of a common law of contracts that treated commercial bargains as the paradigm and promises based on other motives as presumptively unenforceable. Justice John James Ormond announced the Supreme Court's decision.

> The inclination of my mind, is, that the loss and inconvenience, which the plaintiff sustained in breaking up, and mov-

8. *Kirksey v. Kirksey*, 8 Ala. 131, 132 (1845).

> ing to the defendant's, a distance of sixty miles, is a sufficient consideration to support the promise, to furnish her with a house, and land to cultivate, until she could raise her family. My brothers, however think, that the promise on the part of the defendant, was a mere gratuity, and that an action will not lie for its breach.

Sister-in-law Kirksey's case rested on community expectations that people should keep their word; Brother-in-law's successful defense invoked the commercial expectation that law limits its concern to the enforcement of arms-length deals, bargained-for exchanges, in the interest of commerce and industry. The path of the law from the one to the other shows the ability of nineteenth-century American judges to remold the law in the interests of society as they understood those interests... and the fact that the great legal changes of the era were, as such changes always must be, costly to some even as they benefitted others.

This isn't a book of legal history, and so we shall not linger over the parallel changes taking place in the law of property, of torts, of agency and business organization, and so on, but if we could, we would see the same pattern. In response to social change, the courts created, often quite self-consciously, what was largely a new substantive body of law wrapped in the forms of common law conservatism, and this new law was oriented in large measure to the needs—or the preferences—of commercial and manufacturing interests. This can be seen clearly in the connection between the rise of industrialism and the transportation revolution of steamships and railroads (on the one hand), and (on the other) the creation of a law of negligence that shielded manufacturers and transportation enterprises from liability for many of the personal injuries their activities caused. But the pattern is evident across all antebellum law. Much of this substantive law survives to the present; put another way, the basic doctrinal framework of what students learn in the first year of law school was created in large measure in the first half of the nineteenth century to address the controversies of that era.

It will not have escaped your notice that one way to characterize the transformation of American law in the long half century leading up to the Civil War is that it had implicitly political themes. There were winners and losers, and at least some of the time judges were conscious that they were making choices among the values the legal system would foster and protect. Another striking aspect of the legal history of the period is the explicit entry of the law and the courts into the overtly political realm of government through the emergence of what today we call *judicial review*. In England, the Blackstonian orthodoxy was that "what the Parliament doth, no authority upon earth can undo."[9] After the Revolution, with remarkable speed and no sustained opposition, it became the American orthodoxy that American courts have the authority and indeed the duty to ignore or set aside legislation or other actions of the "political" branches of government when, in the judges' view, political actors have violated a written American constitution.

Modern lawyers sometimes believe a host of urban legends about the origins of judicial review, and I don't want you to fall prey to that sort of myth-making. Judicial review of governmental action was not new: for centuries the common law courts had asserted the power to determine whether other tribunals or the officers of the crown were acting lawfully—the power of Common Pleas to do so was of course the very issue that Lord Coke and the Archbishop of Canterbury were debating on that afternoon in 1608 when King James lost his temper. To be sure, the courts generally treated acts of the sovereign King-in-Parliament as beyond their power to question, but after the American Revolution denied sovereignty to any institution of government, and the Revolutionaries wrote written constitutions to set out the powers of government, most lawyers, judges, and politicians quickly came to the conclusion that even legislation could be measured by Coke's "golden Metwand" of the law, and thus a statute's lawfulness under the written constitution could be challenged in court. By the time a certain case every American law student encounters at some point, *Marbury v. Madison*, was decided by the US Supreme Court in 1803, the outright rejection of judicial review of legislation was an extreme position.[10]

---

9. 1 Blackstone, *Commentaries* *160–61.

10. *Marbury v. Madison*, 5 U.S. (1 Cranch) 137 (1803). A year before *Marbury*, when a Jeffersonian Republican denied the legitimacy of judicial review in a congressional debate, Federalist critics seized on the denial as a demonstration that the Republicans were faithless to the Constitution, while other Republicans were at pains to indicate that their imprudent colleague did not speak for the party. *See* H. Jefferson Powell, *A Community Built on Words: The Constitution in History and Politics* 73–85 (rev. ed. 2005) (discussing the episode).

The era's near consensus that a court need not follow a law it found unconstitutional didn't mean that constitutional rulings against government were all that common, but it did raise the political salience of the courts, and it drew attention, both admiring and critical, to the judges. Vested, at least potentially, with the awesome responsibility of speaking truth to power in the people's name, American judges, both state and federal, came to a general public awareness that perhaps no English judge other that Edward Coke had ever enjoyed. Looking back from the end of the century, our friend Oliver Wendell Holmes asked himself whom he would identify to symbolize the whole course of American law up to 1900. Skipping over any number of legal figures whom he more admired in substance, Holmes named a judge whose reputation did not principally lie in the common law developments that Holmes himself thought the most significant for American society. Instead, Holmes picked a lawyer whose fame stemmed from his role in "the rise of a new body of jurisprudence, by which guiding principles are raised above the reach of statute and state"—Chief Justice Marshall of the US Supreme Court. "I do fully believe that if American law were to be represented by a single figure, sceptic and worshipper alike would agree without dispute that the figure could be but one alone, and that one John Marshall."[11]

Marshall's preeminence, as Holmes pointed out, was mostly symbolic—his actual constitutional decisions, including his greatest opinion, *McCulloch v. Maryland* in 1819, were mostly rearguard actions against political developments Marshall thought wrong, and often unsuccessful in their political import—but what Marshall symbolizes is the dramatically greater role of the courts in both public and private life.[12] It was shortly after Marshall's death that the great French observer of US politics, Alexis de Tocqueville, famously wrote that "[t]here is hardly a political question in the United States which does not sooner or later

11. Holmes, John Marshall (1901) in *The Essential Holmes* 208–09. For more on Marshall, see the endnote.

12. *McCulloch v. Maryland*, 17 U.S. (4 Wheat.) 316 (1819), upheld Congress's power to create a national bank. In 1832, President Andrew Jackson expressly denied the authority of *McCulloch* in vetoing on constitutional grounds a bill renewing the bank's charter. For a generation, Congress made no further attempt to create a national banking system.

turn into a judicial one."[13] Tocqueville's insight applies just as much to the manifold changes in so-called private law in this period as it does to the occasional constitutional decision: keep that in mind and you will understand more fully not only *McCulloch v. Maryland* but *Kirksey v. Kirksey* as well.

If we focus not on iconic significance but on immediate, practical impact, we might well locate Chief Justice Marshall's importance in an aspect of his judicial work that Holmes only hinted at. In discussing Marshall's personal virtues, Holmes remarked that in comparison with the Federalist Papers, he "should feel a greater doubt whether Marshall's work proved more than a strong intellect, a good style, personal ascendancy on his court, courage, justice and the convictions of his party." There is a faint air of condescension here—though I find it hard to read "a strong intellect, courage and justice" as an insult!—but I want to focus on two other phrases: Marshall, according to Holmes, had "a good style and personal ascendancy on his court." Holmes's observations, both of which are accurate, reflect a striking if not original feature of Marshall's own practice as a judge. Marshall's predecessor, Chief Justice Oliver Ellsworth, had achieved some success in his short tenure (1796–1800) in persuading his colleagues not to deliver separate opinions but to unite, whenever possible, behind a single "opinion of the Court." Marshall, who sat on the Supreme Court from 1801 to 1835, made Ellsworth's preference the norm. This was a striking change in Anglo-American judicial process. You will recall that the medieval yearbooks were records of conversations among the advocates and judges, and even after the yearbooks gave way to judicial reports in our sense, what was chiefly reported were individual statements by individual judges: there was no single opinion with unique authority as a regular or presumptive matter, a practice that continues, in part, in the English legal system today. By the time Marshall died, however, most American appellate courts had followed his lead.[14]

13. Alexis de Toqueville, *Democracy in America* (J.P. Mayer & Max Lerner eds., George Lawrence trans., 1966) (1835).

14. I suspect that this widely held view overstates the extent to which Marshall himself changed people's minds as opposed to being simply the most prominent practitioner of a custom that enhances a court's power and thus would commend itself to many judges. But there is no reason to doubt that Marshall's example played a role. The Holmes quotation is from his address on Marshall, in *The Essential Holmes* 208.

The invention of the opinion of the Court has some obvious consequences for legal process. For lawyers or judges in later cases, it changes how one states the reasoning for which a case stands. Instead of trying to work out the authoritative meaning of a decision from the possibly conflicting statements of individual judges, one can simply look to a single, authoritative exposition of what "the Court" said the reasoning was. In a later chapter, we'll see why that can have both advantages and disadvantages from a lawyer's perspective; for now, the point is that words announced to be *the* opinion of the Court *as an institution* are by virtue of that label far more easily taken as authoritative in their own right than the thoughts of an individual judge, however distinguished. The idea of precedent became central in both England and the United States in the nineteenth century in ways it had not been before, but only in this country do judicial opinions become authoritative texts in themselves, their precise language invested with much the same gravity as the words of a statute or constitutional provision.

There is every reason to assume that Marshall knew and intended to add weight to his Court's decisions through the Olympian opinion-of-the-Court device that Ellsworth had pioneered; Marshall's cousin and arch-enemy Thomas Jefferson got the point and spent two decades complaining: "An opinion is huddled up in Conclave, perhaps by a majority of one, as if unanimous, delivered [by] a crafty Chief judge, as if unanimous, and, with the silent acquiescence of lazy or timid associates, he sophisticates the law to his mind, by the turn of his own reasoning."[15] Jefferson's criticisms were unavailing, and the *ex cathedra* pronouncement of law "by the Court" was the means by which many of the nineteenth century's innovations were communicated in state as well as federal courts.

Marshall's successors, on his court and elsewhere, have seldom enjoyed his success at minimizing the publication of separate concurrences and dissents. The ideal of a single, authoritative judicial statement, however, is a fixture of twenty-first century American law that shapes even those decisions that actually include no opinion of the Court. Take *National Federation of Independent Business v. Sebelius*, the well-known 2012 US Supreme Court decision addressing two key provisions of the

15. Jefferson, Letter to Thomas Ritchie (Dec. 25, 1820), https://founders.archives.gov/documents/Jefferson/03-16-02-0394.

Affordable Care Act. Chief Justice Roberts announced the judgment of the Court and gave a lengthy statement of his reasons for thinking that judgment correct. In a legal world without our Marshallian legacy, the existence of three other opinions in the case would have no determinative significance: a lawyer trying to restate what *Sebelius* means might look to the arguments in all four opinions in constructing her own account of that meaning. In our actual legal world, the one Marshall helped shape, she ought to begin by figuring out which bits of Roberts's opinion were joined by four other justices and thus are "the opinion of the Court," and which were not, and at some point she would have to worry about the significance of the fact that four other justices signed an opinion ignoring the chief justice entirely despite agreeing with him almost entirely on the two major issues.[16] Marshall's legacy to us, like Chancellor Kent's, is a complex one.

Slavery and the Law's Failure

Up to this point, I have made only one brief allusion to the political and legal issue that came to overshadow everything else in the antebellum United States: the existence of human chattel slavery, imposed only on a single group, defined by race and increasingly confined to the Southern part of the nation. Almost no one in the founding era denied

16. *See National Federation of Independent Business v. Sebelius*, 567 U.S. 519 (2012). The reporter summarized the breakdown in this way: "ROBERTS, C.J., announced the judgment of the Court and delivered the opinion of the Court with respect to Parts I, II, and III-C, in which GINSBURG, BREYER, SOTOMAYOR, and KAGAN, JJ., joined; an opinion with respect to Part IV, in which BREYER and KAGAN, JJ., joined; and an opinion with respect to Parts III-A, III-B, and III-D. GINSBURG, J., filed an opinion concurring in part, concurring in the judgment in part, and dissenting in part, in which SOTOMAYOR, J., joined, and in which BREYER and KAGAN, JJ., joined as to Parts I, II, III, and IV. SCALIA, KENNEDY, THOMAS, and ALITO, JJ., filed a dissenting opinion. THOMAS, J., filed a dissenting opinion." *Id.* at 528–29. Even this understates the complications. The introduction to the chief justice's opinion included a substantial discussion of constitutional first principles, *id.* at 532–38, that a distinguished state judge called "fair, neutral, impartial and nonpartisan," and yet was joined by none of Robert's colleagues. *See* [Wisconsin Supreme Court Chief Justice] Shirley S. Abrahamson, Chief Justice Roberts' message lost on many critics (July 17, 2012), http://host.madison.com/ct/news/opinion/column/chief-justice-shirley-s-abrahamson-chief-justice-roberts-key-message/article_726540dc-cf53-11e1-a811-001a4bcf887a.html.

in theory that slavery was a moral evil, and most of the signers of the Declaration of Independence probably shared its drafter's wishful thinking that somehow slavery would disappear without causing them, or their economic interests, any distress. Any possibility that might occur throughout the country disappeared with the invention of the cotton gin in the 1790s; even the chance that slavery might wither in the upper South had evaporated by 1830, when a last gasp of eighteenth-century anti-slavery idealism failed to overcome the power of financial self-interest and racial antagonism in a Virginia state convention. Slavery would not disappear, it turned out, through the ordinary social and political processes of change.

What about the law? Could the courts have abolished slavery by judicial decree? It seems unlikely that the political system would have tolerated such a decision in a state where slavery was profitable, even if the judges had wanted to abolish slavery, which most of them didn't. The closest a court came to doing so in a state where slavery mattered economically was in Virginia in 1806, in a case called *Hudgins v. Wright*. *Hudgins* was a suit for freedom by a woman named Jackey Wright who claimed that she and her children could not be held in slavery because they were Native American, not African, in ancestry. The trial judge was Chancellor George Wythe, elderly but instinctively radical in his legal and political views. Wythe ruled in Wright's favor, reasoning that under the state's declaration of rights the law presumes that all persons are free, a presumption that might have collapsed slavery in Virginia in short order if applied as Wythe had done.

On appeal, Wythe's judgment was affirmed because Wright and her children were white in appearance, but the state high court expressly rejected Wythe's constitutional reasoning. One of the judges was someone we've already met, St. George Tucker, the editor of "Tucker's Blackstone." Tucker was a rarity in Virginia, a public figure who not only claimed to oppose slavery but was publicly vocal on the question, but Wythe's reasoning was too much even for an emancipation activist in 1806 Virginia: Tucker explained in his opinion that the declaration of rights was "notoriously framed" with eye toward the issue of slavery, and was not intended "by a side wind, to overturn the rights of property." Slavery would not disappear, it turned out, by judicial decree.[17]

17. *Hudgins v. Wright*, 11 Va. (1 Hen. & M.) 134, 141 (1806) (Tucker, J., concurring). Wythe's opinion is lost, but the reporters summarized it in *id.* at 134.

The law of courts and judges, furthermore, did not simply fail to address slavery's existence. An institution of such social and economic importance, where it existed, could not simply escape the notice of the bench and bar: to exist, slavery needed a legal definition, and the law obliged. The most honest, and perhaps most chilling, example of a court meeting that systemic necessity was an 1829 North Carolina Supreme Court decision, *State v. Mann*. The defendant had shot and severely wounded a woman named Lydia whose services as a slave he had leased, and a jury convicted him of a "cruel and unwarrantable" battery. State law was clear that the unwarrantable killing of an enslaved person was criminal; in *Mann*, the question was what other limits the law imposed on the use of violence against a slave by her master. The state argued that the master/slave relation was like other asymmetrical legal relationships (parent/child, etc.) and that in all such relationships the law required that the person in authority act reasonably and without unnecessary cruelty.

Writing for the court, Judge Thomas Ruffin swept aside the state's argument. "The Court does not recognize the application [of this principle]. There is no likeness between the cases."

> It may well be asked, which power of the master accords with right? The answer will probably sweep them all away. But we cannot look at the matter in that light. The truth is that we are forbidden to enter upon a train of general reasoning on the subject. We cannot allow the right of the master to be brought into discussion in courts of justice.

Slavery, in other words, created an area of social life into which legal reason could not go, within which violence was unchecked by law. While the legislature could, by an act of political will, modify this reality, Ruffin denied the competence of law to do so. "The difficulty is determining where a Court may properly begin.... The Court, therefore, disclaims the power of changing the relation in which these parts of our people stand to each other." If law is reason that measures the exercise of power, then slavery as Ruffin portrayed it was anti-law, a system of power that excluded reason.[18]

---

18. *State v. Mann*, 13 N.C. (2 Dev.) 263, 265–67 (1820) (cleaned up). Opponents of slavery described *Mann* as "solemnly from the bench announcing th[e] great foundation principle of slavery." Harriet Beecher Stowe, *The Key to Uncle Tom's Cabin* 133 (1854).

The question that increasingly engaged the attention of some lawyers from the 1820s on was whether the law could end or at least ameliorate the political and moral controversies surrounding slavery. What you thought counted as an improvement, to be sure, almost always depended on whether you were pro- or anti-slavery: it was in this period that the founders' vague disapproval of the institution was increasingly displaced by attitudes that were either more fervently opposed or more insistently supportive. Opponents of slavery turned to Northern state legislatures, many of which enacted personal liberty laws that interfered with the federal statute requiring the return of fugitive slaves. For those lawyers who accepted slavery as inevitable or even desirable, law's possible contribution to the controversy over slavery lay, unsurprisingly, in a very different direction, with the elaboration of doctrinal and conceptual safeguards for slavery that reached their height in the infamous *Dred Scott* decision of 1857.[19]

Chief Justice Roger Brooke Taney's lead opinion in *Dred Scott*—he filed it as the opinion of the Court although it has never been clear whether that was an entirely accurate characterization—reached the conclusion that Black Americans were constitutionally barred from citizenship. Taney did so, however, only by misrepresenting historical facts and ignoring previous decisions and the contrary views of earlier jurists like Chancellor Kent. Furthermore, in dicta Taney attempted to resolve the most heated national political issue of the day—the extension of slavery to federal territories—by denying to Congress any power to restrict it. Taney no doubt intended *Dred Scott* to dampen down sectional conflict by constitutionalizing slavery's status, but its consequences were quite the opposite: in the decision's wake, the anti-slavery-expansion Republican party won the presidential election of 1860, prompting secession, Civil War, and the abolition of slavery.

Taney's *Dred Scott* opinion displays the extent to which an individual lawyer can employ institutional position and professional skill as unscrupulous means to an utterly unworthy goal. But there are broader conclusions to be drawn. There are political limits to the law as a means of achieving even the worthiest end: a Supreme Court filled with nine Chancellor Wythes could not have decreed emancipation in 1857 and seen its order obeyed. But even when a moral or social wrong is so great

19. *Scott v. Sandford*, 16 U.S. (19 How.) 393 (1857).

that fully addressing it requires an act of political will on the part of the community as a whole, lawyers and judges have choices to make in the American legal system. As E.P. Thompson wrote, the rule of law is "an unqualified human good," but we must not be starry-eyed about the way the legal system functions in practice. Tucker was sincerely opposed to the institution of slavery, Taney was its enthusiastic defender, but *Hudgins* no less than *Dred Scott* treated persons who were in fact part of the community as if they were not, and thus beyond the protection of the law.[20]

Ruffin's opinion in *State v. Mann* raises what is perhaps an even more disturbing possibility, that lawyers and judges may recognize a social or moral evil, recognize further that evil's contradiction to the rule of law, and yet think the legal system helpless to resist. Unlike Tucker and Taney, Ruffin acknowledged that that the line separating slavery from freedom divided North Carolinians, "these parts of *our people*," and thus created a zone of anti-law beyond the reach of "the Golden metwand and measure" of power that Coke had lauded. In any event, the responses of Tucker and Ruffin and Taney to slavery were not unavoidable; they were choices, decisions by highly intelligent lawyers to move the law in practice further away from the ideal that Thompson described as the imposition of "effective inhibitions upon power and the defense" of the individual against "power's all-intrusive claims."

The Formalization of American Law, ca. 1870 to ca. 1930

The previous section of this chapter may read as if I were painting a portrait of American law around 1860 as trapped in a dead end, and that is quite intentional: for all its successes in the early Republic, I think the American legal system, and the political system of which it was a part, had driven into a cul de sac from which there were no outlets and there was no turning back. Slavery would disappear, it turned out, but not

20. Thompson, *Whigs and Hunters* 266. *See Hudgins*, 11 Va. (1 Hen. & M.) at 141 (Tucker, J., concurring) (referring to Black Virginians as "those very people whom we have been compelled from imperious circumstances to retain, generally, in the same state of bondage that they were in at the revolution, in which they had no *concern, agency* or *interest*").

through ordinary politics or the orderly processes of the law: it would take war and hundreds of thousands of lives to end the institution. The Civil War was followed, to be sure, by a burst of constitutional and statutory lawmaking that provided the legal framework for Reconstruction, but those changes looked at first, briefly, like a revolutionary reboot of the entire system rather than a continuation of the past: in an 1873 opinion, for example, Justice Noah Swayne described the Reconstruction era constitutional amendments as "a new departure.... Fairly construed these amendments may be said to rise to the dignity of a new Magna Charta."[21]

This book cannot pause over the complex and often tragic events that followed the adoption of the Reconstruction amendments and resulted very quickly in the neutralization of much of the idealism Swayne found in them. (The words I just quoted were written in dissent.) If we could, we would find striking parallels between the partial dismantling of Reconstruction after the Civil War and the surrender to evil before the war that we traced in the decisions of Tucker and Ruffin and Taney. Once again, judges and lawyers made choices with lamentable consequences, largely by attempting to minimize the legal significance of the changes wrought by the war, Emancipation, and the amendments.[22] Instead, I will simply observe that history never stands still: the American legal system of, say, 1900 was significantly different from the legal system of 1847, when Chancellor Kent died. What the courts and the bar were able to do was ensure that the late nineteenth century's changes from antebellum law had less to do with the great events of mid-century than with developments within the law itself.

The central difference between American law in the first half of the nineteenth century and at the end of the century is often characterized as a turn to "formalism" in legal decision making. This characterization of the changes is usually part of a broader account of American legal history. Put a bit oversimply, that story goes like this. In the beginning American law was enormously pragmatic, creative, oriented toward serving society's needs, its history "a romp through the garden of Eden" characterized by "the happy sight of great judges deciding great cases

21. *Slaughter-House Cases*, 83 U.S. (16 Wall.) 36, 125 (1872) (Swayne, J., dissenting).

22. The opinion of the Court with which Justice Swayne was disagreeing commented that "we do not see in those amendments any purpose to destroy the main features of the general system," an unfair misdescription of the dissenters' views which the majority used to justify its very narrow reading of the amendments. *Id.* at 82.

greatly." After the Civil War, the law lost its way, abandoned the search for socially useful principles based on experience in favor of a search for the logically correct rules derived from formal conceptual schemes. Or, in a word, lawyers and judges succumbed to formalism, the dark night of the law. In the darkness, however, a few lights shone brightly—Oliver Wendell Holmes and later Benjamin N. Cardozo—and after their Legal Realist followers in the 1920s and early 30s, American law returned to the pragmatism and, well, realism of the early period but with a much greater sophistication.[23] This story isn't entirely wrong-headed: for example, the early nineteenth century was in many respects a tremendously creative period in American law, so long as we ignore its utter failure in dealing with the moral evil of slavery (a big ask, one might think). But even so, the story is partial, one-sided, and ultimately relies on erroneous premises in reaching misleading conclusions.

The problems begin with the story's loaded use of words. Formalism is not a four-letter word, and pragmatism (or realism) is not an automatic virtue. The great antebellum judges and lawyers, Kent and Marshall and Story, and even lesser lights such as Justice Ormond of *Kirksey v. Kirksey*, were scarcely hostile to arguments based on precedent or formal legal categories. As we've already noted, it was the lawyers of that time who created the substantive concepts and categories of law—contract and property and tort and so on—that finally supplanted the largely medieval procedural forms as the way lawyers learned and organized their thinking about the law to this day. The post-Civil War course of American law was not a sudden lapse into some radically inferior way of thinking: it would be fairer to say that in most ways it saw the further development, at an increasingly more sophisticated level, of the intellectual trends before the war.

More basically, the story's tendentious opposition of pragmatism (Good) to formalism (Bad) is simply wrong. It is of the very nature of law, as understood in both the common law and civil law traditions, that it consists of formalized rules and principles that guide decision making even if they do not dictate particular decisions. And legal rules very often

---

23. The quotation and imagery are drawn from Grant Gilmore's engaging, imaginative, often insightful, but sometimes wildly idiosyncratic book *The Ages of American Law*. *See* Gilmore & Bobbitt, *Ages* 37. Gilmore took a rather different view of Holmes, Cardozo, and the Realists, but in other respects his book is an especially pure retelling of the tale I summarize in the text.

do just that: whatever else may be said about my driving, I am not violating a 55 mph speed limit if I am driving 50. In his *The Common Law*, Holmes repeatedly insisted that the history of English law displayed a continuous development from subjective to objective, and thus became increasingly formalized; from its beginnings, American law has followed its English parent in using formal modes of thought to identify legal procedures, as well as the hierarchies of legal authority and legal institutions.

Conversely, the disposition to adopt legal rules that are pragmatically justifiable because they realistically address the needs of society is self-evidently a good thing only if one agrees with what the decision makers see as society's needs, and with their approach to legal problems. As we saw earlier in this chapter, choices among legal rules and principles are implicitly political; they regularly require the decision maker to favor one set of interests over another, and thus some people's preferences over other people's. Strict rules about negligence liability probably were wise and pragmatic from the perspective of the factory owner or railroad company. Not so much for their employees and passengers. Formalized rules are often necessary if the rule of law is to impose effective limitations on power.

Leaving aside the problem with the nomenclature, the claim that post-Civil War American law was formalistic—in this story the negative connotations of that word are clear—or reflected a general move from pragmatism to formalism that then was reversed sometime around 1930 assumes a sharp dichotomy that actual American legal history belies and that isn't even possible in a legal system in the common law tradition. The law is always permeated by formalized rules and principles, not just in statutes and other "written law" authorities (where that is obvious) but in judicial precedent and doctrine as well. And (equally) no sophisticated lawyer has ever thought that law is a system of concepts freely spinning on its own in an intellectual vacuum entirely unrelated to the social and political realities of society. Formalism and pragmatism are *always and simultaneously* aspects of common law thinking.

The historical truth in the tale of American law's adoption and subsequent rejection of formalism rests on the reality at a given point in time it may be possible to detect a tendency—perhaps most clearly among leading members of bench and bar and influential commentators, but percolating throughout the profession—to put more emphasis on formal thought than pragmatic arguments or vice versa.

> Law is a particular way of using texts and precedents, and there are many ways of using these tools. It is an empirical rather than a theoretical question as to which techniques of using precedent prevail in any particular historical context. In some contexts, lawyers and judges use texts to generate rules. In other historical contexts, the practice of using texts and precedents yields a process of practical judgments about what is good for social well-being.[24]

Thus, what we can say about American law from about 1870 through the 1920s is that much of that time the emphasis in American legal thought tended toward formalism. But to say more than that is simply a mistake, as is any suggestion that in making this limited empirical observation we are thereby condemning what we are observing.

An important cause of this heightened emphasis on formal modes of thought was the expanding role of American legislatures in this period. Legal development in the antebellum period generally took place in the courts, but by the late nineteenth century both Congress and the state legislatures were increasingly taking the lead in crafting legislative solutions to perceived social problems. State legislation addressed a wide range of economic, social, and health issues, with different legislatures sometimes taking very different approaches.[25] The arrival of peacetime federal regulation can be precisely dated, with the enactment of the Interstate Commerce Act of 1887 and the Sherman Antitrust Act of 1890.

---

24. L.H. LaRue, Constitutional Law and Constitutional History 36 Buffalo L. Rev. 373, 399–400 (1987). In this brilliant essay, Professor LaRue had constitutional law specifically in mind, but his point is generally true in the common law tradition.

25. As one scholar nicely summarized "the tremendous flurry of state activity that followed on the heels of the Civil War":

> States enacted laws ensuring the purity of foods, liquors, and medicines; promoting or requiring vaccination; establishing minimum requirements for certain professions (such as teaching, medicine, pharmacy, dentistry, and law); requiring public inspection of the accounts of banks, insurance companies, mutual aid organizations, and railroad companies; and prohibiting monopolies. States also tackled the "labor question," mandating inspection of factories, regulating wages and work contracts, and restricting the working hours and conditions of children, women, and, in some cases, men. Before 1897, state legislatures passed more than sixteen hundred laws regulating the terms of labor.

Susan J. Pearson, A New Birth of Regulation: The State of the State After the Civil War, 5 J. Civ. War Era 422, 423–24 (2015).

The 1887 statute created the first real peacetime (federal) regulatory agency, the Interstate Commerce Commission, while the Sherman Act extended federal authority over economic activity previously regulated inconsistently by the states or not at all. An ever-growing part of both state and federal court dockets in the period was taken up with questions of statutory construction and application that demanded formal interpretive analyses rather than common-law analogical reasoning. And as statutory law assumed greater prominence, the domain in which courts were free to make decisions on a common law basis shrank.[26]

An increased tendency to employ formalism in resolving legal issues can be seen in late nineteenth century common law decisions as well in two respects, the first being in the profession's understanding of *stare decisis*, the rule of precedent. Medieval and early modern common lawyers had lots of judge-made law but no rigid rule about adherence to precedent, and generally viewed the principle of *stare decisis* as fully applicable only to an established *line* of decisions. Antebellum US lawyers generally agreed. They invoked precedent happily, but often as a means to a just end rather than a limitation on reaching that end. By the end of the century, lawyers and judges generally understood a decision by the highest court in a jurisdiction as entitled to the full weight of precedent, and treated adherence to precedent as a point of judicial virtue.

In addition to displaying an enhanced or stricter view of *stare decisis*, American law in the period between 1870 and 1930 saw the full unfolding of the impulse to systematize and thus formalize general concepts and theories of tort, contract, and so on that had appeared earlier in Chancellor Kent's *Commentaries* and Justice Story's expositions of specific areas of law and their antebellum progeny. This was the era of the great academic treatise that reorganizes an entire field of law into a coherent and logically consistent architecture of principles and rules—Bigelow on

---

26. It's worth noting that the common law's domain did not shrink at the same pace that new legislation expanded the areas of law a legislature intended to govern by statute for two reasons. First, most American courts adhered to the old English canon of statutory construction that statutes in derogation of the common law are to be strictly construed, and thus sought to minimize legislative "interference" with judge-made law by narrow construction of statutory language. Second, many courts were increasingly ready to invalidate legislation under state constitutions or the Fourteenth Amendment. As a practical matter, the derogation canon was probably the bigger obstacle to legislation. *See id.* at 424 ("State courts upheld the vast majority of regulatory and protective legislation.").

Torts (the 1891 edition), Wigmore on Evidence (1904), Williston on Contracts (1920–22). A great deal of what contemporary law students study stems directly from the doctrinal systems perfected in this period.

On the surface, these commitments to comprehensive theories and to adherence to precedent might seem to be in tension. Kent, you will recall, found himself "embarrassed" by some precedent or technical rule only "once in a while," but I assume he hoped that readers of his *Commentaries* would generally follow his exposition of the law even if they disagreed. What unites the two impulses is that each makes possible a greater degree of formalism in legal thought and decision. Precedents and general theories of liability play a similar role in modern common law to that of legislative text in cases controlled by statute. They impose discipline on judicial creativity, and create professional benchmarks against which to measure the faithfulness of today's decision to yesterday's law. It is formalism to decide that reliance on a promise does not make the promisor liable in contract because an earlier case so held rather than because in this individual case, all things considered, that is the most just outcome, but the decision is often no worse for that. Formalism makes for stability and predictability in the law, it facilitates adherence to the principle that all parties should be treated the same, and it limits the degree to which individual judges can indulge their own, perhaps idiosyncratic, sense of justice or political preference.

In 1887, a case came before the Alabama Supreme Court in which the plaintiff alleged facts strikingly similar to those of *Kirksey v. Kirksey* forty years earlier: the plaintiff claimed that he had given up the idea of moving to Texas in reliance on a promise that if he stayed in Alabama the promisor would pay his debts. The outcome in the 1887 case, *Head v. Baldwin*, was the same as in *Kirksey*, but in reaching that conclusion, the court relied on one of the requirements of the reigning theory of contract, mutuality of obligation, and the precedent set by *Kirksey v. Kirksey* itself. The issue, as the 1887 court saw it, was not whether it would be just to impose liability on the defendant, or if a rule allowing the plaintiff to recover would be socially beneficial: the court's duty was to decide whether the plaintiff's allegations fit within the legal formal concept of "contract" and the court's own precedent. In *Head*, the incipient formalism of *Kirksey* had become full-fledged, self-conscious adherence to reigning legal theory.[27]

---

27. *Head v. Baldwin*, 83 Ala. 132 (1887).

As I have suggested, the reason formalism played such a major role in this period was in part the pragmatic value (!) of formal approaches to legal reasoning. Two aspects of the institutional context for formalism's attractiveness played an important role as well: the explosion in the availability of case law, and the creation of the modern American law school. A common law system in which judge-made precedent is important needs to find a way to make the precedents known and accessible, and this was a serious problem for American lawyers in the Revolutionary and founding era. There were no published reports of colonial American decisions, and access to English case law was spotty and incomplete; one reason for the enormous success of Blackstone's *Commentaries* and Tucker's Blackstone was that they could substitute for the missing precedents.

Soon after independence, however, American lawyers began addressing this problem. From the 1790s on there were both official and unofficial reports of American decisions, and the early 1800s saw the rise of case law digests, often unsystematic and always unutterably boring attempts to summarize decisions across jurisdictions, and thus make the decisions available for lawyers and judges outside the few cities with comprehensive law libraries. But by the late nineteenth century the problem was exactly the reverse: bench and bar were beginning to drown in an ever-growing sea of reported decisions, to the alarm of leading American lawyers. We can identify the exact year in which this problem became a crisis: 1879, the year that saw the publication of the first volume of what became West Publishing Company's National Reporter System, covering all the states and the federal courts as well, and giving lawyers access to an organized presentation of essentially all the American appellate caselaw everywhere. No problem now of being wrong-footed by opposing counsel who had discovered the controlling case in a source you didn't know, or (if you were a judge) of finding that there were no precedents in your state's official reports: if your state had never addressed a *Kirksey v. Kirksey* problem, the West regional reporters would find you ten that had. In this fashion, "the West Publishing Company, whose interest in jurisprudential theory [we] assume to have been minimal, made a contribution to our legal history which, in its importance, may have dwarfed the contributions of Langdell, Holmes, and all the learned professors on all the great law faculties."[28] But the obvious

28. Gilmore & Bobbitt, *Ages* 53.

effect of this "contribution" was to increase exponentially the problem of making sense of the now endless series of cases.

Holmes we have met; we now need to make the acquaintance of Christopher Columbus Langdell, who served as dean of the Harvard Law School from 1870 to 1895, and whose name is synonymous with the creation of the current system of legal education in this country. When Langdell became dean, law schools were either small businesses run as a sideline enterprise by judges or practicing lawyers or, as at Harvard, loosely structured lecture courses affiliated with a college whose student bodies waxed and waned in size largely in response to the college's success in attracting some famous lawyer to give the lectures; the vast majority of American lawyers studied for the bar in a practitioner's office and never attended a single class. By the time Dean Langdell retired, the modern university law school was an important presence in the profession, although it would still take several decades for possession of a law degree to become mandatory in most states for admission to the bar.

Langdell's personal role in this remarkable development was extensive, in part because of Harvard's national reputation but also as a result of his energetic promotion of his ideas, both pedagogical and substantive. For Langdell, the law was a science, the library its laboratory, the cases the subjects for experimentation. The year after he became dean, he published the first law school casebook, on contracts. In the introduction, he explained that the "cases which are useful and necessary... bear an exceedingly small proportion to all that have been reported. The vast majority are useless and worse than useless for any purpose of systematic study."[29] His casebook, in other words, was devoted to what Langdell thought was the True Theory of contract law, and did not risk misleading the student by exposing him to error; the Socratic method in the law school classroom (which Langdell also introduced) owes its inquisitorial nature to Langdell's determination to eliminate heretical misunderstandings by the students. Shortly afterward, Langdell wrote what was in effect the first law school teacher's manual, designed to ensure that other professors didn't stray from the truth either. Both the casebook and the Socratic method were adopted for other subjects and at other schools in short order.

---

29. Christopher Columbus Langdell, *A Selection of Cases on the Law of Contracts* vi (1871).

Langdell's other great innovation was to re-orient law teaching from an avocation of the bench and bar to a serious university discipline. Instead of looking for some famous judge with scholarly interests—Harvard's greatest professor prior to Langdell had been Justice Story, moonlighting from his day job—henceforth, law schools increasingly hired their professors on the basis not of experience in practice but of academic firepower.[30] The intellectual quality of both teaching and scholarship went up rapidly (there were very few Professor-Justice Storys!), and the prestige of the law professor followed suit. Langdell and his imitators left for another day the question whether at some point academic law risks becoming too remote from law in practice.

The Langdellian revolution in legal education had important consequences both institutional and substantive. If we could take a time machine and attend Dean Langdell's retirement dinner, the resemblance between his institution and the twenty-first century law school would be startling. The common 1L curriculum was already in place (with, to be sure, the non-trivial omission of legal research and writing, and constitutional law); the casebook had supplanted the hornbook as the usual student text; in the classroom there were fewer and fewer lectures, and more and more cold calls and professorial demands to state the facts in X v. Y; those professors increasingly thought of themselves primarily as scholars and teachers rather than as members of the bar; the student-edited law review was on its way to becoming the paradigmatic American form of legal literature.

The university law school also played its own role in substantive legal change. Understandably enough, the new-style Langdellian law professor, who had little experience in practice but was hired precisely because of his academic abilities, was usually more interested in ideas than in the immediate concerns of the practitioner. The conceptual and formal demands of *stare decisis* and the idea of a True Theory were as congenial to him as to most judges of the era, and the roles of the courts and the schools in cultivating a formalist mindset were mutually reenforcing. As an ever-larger percentage of the elite bar, and eventually of the profession generally, came to the law through law school, the idea that law is a rigorously deductive science with demonstrable right and wrong an-

30. It would be an overstatement to suggest that the life of the modern American law school has not been experience but logic.

swers reached by the proper application of the appropriate intellectual tools took hold far beyond Harvard.

The increasingly prestigious law faculties of the leading law schools also played their role in the efforts of the bench and bar to deal with the unanticipated consequence of the West National Reporter System: that there was now available far too much precedent, much of it simply wrong from the standpoint of judges, litigators, and professors committed to what the American Bar Association (organized in 1878) called "the advancement of the science of jurisprudence, the promotion of the administration of justice and a uniformity of legislation throughout the country." By the careful selection of which decisions to include, the casebook editor could inculcate in his students a clear sense of the right answers and the True Theory, and Langdellian treatises and law review articles were powerful tools for "the advancement of the science of jurisprudence."[31]

As for "uniformity of legislation," in the last decade of the century, the leaders of the ABA engineered the establishment of the National Conference of Commissioners on Uniform State Laws, a body dedicated to the formulation and proposal to state legislators of partial codifications of the law. The commissioners were state appointees, the drafters of the model laws were usually professors, and in the early decades their work followed the lines, needless to say, of the relevant True Theory and the approved precedents. The uniform laws were, therefore, in substance, what leading judges and law professors thought the common law ought to be. The conference was highly productive and enjoyed amazing successes, notably with the Uniform Sales Act drafted by Harvard Professor Samuel Williston and formally proposed by the commission in 1906. The Sales Act was eventually superseded by the Uniform Commercial Code, first proposed in 1952 and now in force in some version in all fifty states, and the conference, now called the Uniform Law Commission, remains active and important.

Yet another collaborative effort of judges, leaders of the organized bar, and elite law schools was the American Law Institute, created in 1923, and constituted by its own election of its members. Just as the uniform laws proposed by the National Conference were meant to encourage the

---

31. *See* History of the American Bar Association, https://www.upcounsel.com/lectl-history-of-the-american-bar-association.

good and forestall the bad in state legislation, so the ALI's most characteristic projects, the Restatements, were intended to provide the bench and bar with the most enlightened and up-to-date versions of the various True Theories and enable lawyers to distinguish correctly decided cases, no matter by whom they were decided, from mistakes. Not all sitting judges were impressed by the pretensions of the ALI's members to dictate the contents of the common law, to be sure: US Supreme Court Justice Louis Brandeis dismissed its first meeting with the withering observation "why, I am restating the law every day."[32] Nevertheless, while some of the Restatements have been duds, the successful ones, by dint of their clarity and cohesion, have decisively shaped the direction of judge-made law in the areas they address.

As I observed earlier, changes in the law are never without their political and social consequences even when those who make them have no express political intentions. We need not doubt the sincerity of the early ABA's nonpartisan and (in a sense) non-ideological commitment to the advancement of legal science and of justice. It is nevertheless true, that what most lawyers understood by the science of jurisprudence and the True Theories of contract and tort had a strongly pro-business and status quo orientation. The same can be said, as you know, of antebellum law, but only up to a point: legal thought in the first half of the century was too experimental and too allergic to dogma to become completely subservient to a rigid theory of society. In contrast, that was precisely what the critics of mainstream law in the decades before and after 1900 thought had happened: from the critics' perspective, the so-called science of law was the translation into legal terms of a harsh Social Darwinism designed to benefit the economically privileged and to undermine democratically enacted reforms.

The question about exactly how far the critics were right has no simple answer, although it seems fair to say that a great deal of both tort and contract law in 1900 was heavily weighted in favor of the interests of big business and against recovery by individual consumers and employees. I should point out as well that the pragmatic effect of the efforts of judges, lawyers, and professors to promote True Theories and uniform laws was to reduce the impact of legislation that looked in other substan-

32. Holmes, Letter to Frederick Pollock (Feb. 24, 1923), in *The Essential Holmes* 217. Holmes's comment: "I am an aged skeptic and was pleased at Brandeis's remark."

tive directions. As mentioned above in a footnote, it is a centuries-old maxim of the common law that statutes passed in derogation of the common law ought to be strictly construed—in other words, the courts should minimize the effects of legislation on the law that judges can control. The elite bar of the period around 1900 turned this maxim into a comprehensive program that began with the first-year curriculum in law school and reached its dramatic high point in decisions such as the famous *Lochner v. New York* (1905) that appeared to the critics to turn common law doctrines into constitutional dogmas unchangeable by ordinary democratic processes. Robert Rantoul, had he been alive, might have said I told you so.

★ ★ ★

We have now arrived back to our old friend Oliver Wendell Holmes. In 1900 Holmes was fifty-nine, chief justice of his home state's high court, a legal scholar with a thoroughly mainstream reputation, and thought to be mildly progressive in his political inclinations, largely on the basis of a couple of decisions in which he had written in defense of the rights of labor to organize in opposition to management. In reality, Holmes cared very little about politics, and his political and economic views were not in the least progressive. For the most part his inclinations in reaching judicial decisions were cautious and mainstream: he was, for example, extremely reluctant to overturn precedent even when he thought it wrong. But in 1900 Holmes still had almost a third of a century of professional work ahead of him: he would shortly move to the US Supreme Court, where he would eventually become a national, widely beloved figure, almost an icon—the "Yankee from Olympus," as a 1944 bestseller called him.[33] Like his reputed progressivism, a lot of Holmes's fame rested more on urban legend than reality, and Holmes's reputation has had several ups and downs since his death, but he is, nevertheless, a crucial figure in the history we have been examining.

Let me give you, briefly, a preview of why this is so. It is partly as a symbol, partly because he really was a significant judge and legal critic, that Holmes can represent the destabilization of the legal world of True

33. *See* Catherine Drinker Bowen, *Yankee from Olympus: Justice Holmes and His Family* (1944).

Theory and legal science that came into being after the Civil War. Holmes was too impatient and too interested in his own thoughts to write treatises analyzing other people's decisions (his 1880 lectures on the common law were to be not only his first but his last real book), and Holmesian legal thought no more involved the wholesale repudiation of Dean Langdell's world than Langdell had nullified the work of Chancellor Kent. But with Holmes, we come to a legal mind that is distinctly modern. In many ways he is clearly our contemporary, in a sense that Kent, or for that matter Langdell, clearly was not. I will have more to say about how Holmes thought about the law—and through him about how you and I cannot help but think—in the next chapter.

In conclusion, Holmes's professional career tells us something important about the formalist legal world that is the intellectual baseline against which Holmes and his followers revolted. Judges and professors sometimes accord the neatly organized legal concepts and theories of Langdell's intellectual universe—contract law simply *is* the law of bargained-for exchanges, and the like—a quality of permanence and stability even when they mean to criticize. But this is an illusion. Holmes became a lawyer before Langdell became a dean, and Langdell's legal world view was on the verge of collapse by the time Holmes reluctantly retired from the bench. In other words, what a distinguished legal historian has called "classical legal thought" barely lasted for a single professional lifetime... although I concede that Holmes's was a very long professional lifetime![34]

34. *See* William M. Wiecek, *The Lost World of Classical Legal Thought* (1998).

FOUR

Thinking Like a (Modern) Lawyer

In 1920, the Yale Law School invited Benjamin N. Cardozo to deliver a series of lectures. Cardozo, a judge on the New York Court of Appeals (the state's highest court), accepted somewhat reluctantly, but the book that came out of his lectures, entitled *The Nature of the Judicial Process*, quickly became famous. Indeed, Cardozo's may well be the most celebrated book on American law after Holmes's *The Common Law*: a waggish critic once said that what the two books have "in common [are] the facts that nobody reads them and everybody praises them."[1] Most readers at the time praised Judge Cardozo, not for his originality so much as for his insight: one reviewer, himself a sitting judge, wrote that there was "nothing new" in *The Nature of the Judicial Process*, but that the book "is as brilliant as it is convincing."[2]

Cardozo was a rising star in the American legal firmament in 1920, and for this reason it is perhaps not surprising that his contemporaries lauded his book. After its publication, Cardozo's reputation only continued to grow; six years after giving his Yale lectures he became chief judge of his court; with him in the center chair the New York Court of Appeals was universally seen as the greatest common law court in the United States. In 1932 Cardozo, a Democrat, was appointed by a Republican president to the US Supreme Court to succeed the aged Justice Holmes on the ground that there was no one else worthy to take Holmes's place. *The Nature of the Judicial Process* enhanced Cardozo's growing personal

---

1. Gilmore & Bobbitt, *Ages* 68.

2. Rousseau A. Burch, Book Review, 31 Yale L.J. 677, 677 (1922). Burch was a justice on the Kansas Supreme Court from 1902 to 1937 (chief justice, 1935–37).

reputation; more importantly, the book and its warm reception were a sign of shifting emphases in American legal thought.[3]

As we discussed in the last chapter, formalist and non-formalist modes of legal thought and argument are not irreconcilably opposed but complementary. *The Nature of the Judicial Process* was not, as it is sometimes misunderstood to be, a signal that a previous era of stark formalism was about to be replaced by a brave new world of realism. Indeed, Cardozo himself meant no such thing. Only three years after he gave the Yale lectures, the American Law Institute would inaugurate its great project of restating the law by formalizing the rules and principles of the common law; Judge Cardozo would himself be in attendance. *The Nature of the Judicial Process* was not an attack on formalism as a tool of legal argument and decision, but it *was* a challenge to the assumption that legal reasoning can exclude elements of choice and creativity, that a judge in particular should approach difficult legal questions as if they were problems in Euclidean geometry with indisputably correct answers.

Cardozo began his first lecture by asking himself the question, "What is it that I do when I decide a case?" I do not think his answer would have reassured Robert Rantoul. Rantoul's attack on judge-made law, indeed, got a gentle back of the hand at once. After asking his question, Cardozo immediately listed a bewildering range of considerations that he as a judge might entertain—not just precedent and logic, but also custom, consequences, the judge's views of social welfare, justice, morals—and simply asserted that "all these ingredients enter in varying proportions into that strange compound which is brewed daily in the caldron of the courts." "I am not concerned to inquire whether judges ought to be allowed to brew such a compound at all. I take judge-made law as one of the existing realities of life."[4]

From Cardozo's perspective, the basic error in criticisms such as Rantoul's lies in a failure to grasp the significance of the fact that legal decisions are *judgments*, decisions made by human beings on issues that often admit of more than one plausible resolution. Still in his first lecture, Cardozo warily quoted Eugen Ehrlich, an Austrian legal scholar, that "In the long run, 'there is no guaranty of justice . . . except the personality of the judge.'" Ehrlich's retreat to an ultimately subjective stan-

3. For more on Cardozo, see the endnote.

4. Cardozo, *The Nature of the Legal Process* 10 (1921).

dard went too far for Cardozo, or better, accepted a sharp dichotomy between the objective and the subjective elements in legal thought that Cardozo thought fallacious. "So far as the distinction has practical significance, the traditions of our jurisprudence commit us to the objective standard." But still, "We may try to see things as objectively as we please. None the less, we can never see them with any eyes but our own. To that test they are all brought—a form of pleading or an act of parliament, the wrongs of paupers or the rights of princes, a village ordinance or a nation's charter." Objectivity is not a characteristic that is to be discovered "out there," already present in the law, the common law in the sense of a transcendental body of law brooding in the sky. For Cardozo, objectivity is, instead, a personal and moral "ideal... to be striven for within the limits of our capacity," all the while realizing that "we cannot transcend the limitations of the ego."[5]

In his final lecture, Cardozo gave a brief account of his own journey away from understanding law as a science in Dean Langdell's sense.

> We like to figure to ourselves the processes of justice as coldly objective and impersonal.... I was much troubled in spirit, in my first years on the bench, to find how trackless was the ocean on which I was embarked. I sought for certainty.... I was trying to reach land, the solid land of fixed and settled rules, the paradise of a justice that would declare itself by tokens plainer and more commanding than its pale and glimmering reflections in my own vacillating mind and conscience.... As the years have gone by... I have become reconciled to the uncertainty, because I have grown to see it as inevitable. I have grown to see that the process in its highest reaches is not discovery but creation... [that] the great tides and currents which engulf the rest of men do not turn aside and pass the judges by... [and that the judge's own "doubts and misgivings, hopes and fears" are part of the process] in which principles that have served their day expire, and new principles are born.[6]

5. *Id.* at 16–17, 106, 13, 106.

6. *Id.* at 166–68 (reordered).

At many places in *The Nature of the Judicial Process* Cardozo was at pains to stress that recognizing the unavoidable personal, creative, subjective element in legal reasoning is entirely consistent with formal and objective decision making...most of the time: "*Stare decisis* is at least the everyday working rule of our law." "The factors of determinism [in the law] cabin and confine within narrow bounds the range of unfettered choice." But in the end, Cardozo was unwilling to pretend that making a decision in law is parallel to solving a problem in geometry. The judge's freedom of decision should be, Cardozo insisted, "informed by tradition, methodized by analogy, [and] disciplined by system." But as he went on to admit, "Wide enough in all conscience is the field of discretion that remains." The lawyer or judge who sees the law with Cardozo's eyes no longer lives, at least not comfortably and in good faith, in the world Langdell imagined. She really has no choice but to live in ours.[7]

★ ★ ★

It's all Holmes's fault. Not really, of course, but there are good reasons for treating Holmes as a symbol, and in part a creator, of the mindset of the modern lawyer. Benjamin Cardozo would have agreed: in his Yale lectures he predicted that it would be to Holmes's opinion in the 1905 *Lochner* case that lawyers "will turn to in the future as the beginning of an era," and in an article published near the older man's retirement, Cardozo called Holmes "the great overlord of [American] law."[8] We need not share Cardozo's reverence to appreciate Holmes's significance, or Holmes's value to us as a window onto the modern legal consciousness. After all, the life of the law has not been logic but experience, and whatever you or I think about Holmes, as lawyers we cannot help but think along lines that he helped lay out. I want to indicate six ways in which I believe we can see in Holmes an important aspect of the twenty-first century legal worldview.

---

7. *Id.* at 20, 170, 141.

8. *Id.* at 79; Cardozo, Mr. Justice Holmes, 44 Harv. L. Rev. 682, 691 (1931). *See Lochner v. New York*, 198 U.S. 45 (1905) (invalidating a maximum-hours law as a violation of freedom of contract). Holmes's famous dissent argued that "This case is decided upon an economic theory which a large part of the country does not entertain.... [The Constitution] is made for people of fundamentally different views." *Id.* at 75–76 (Holmes, J., dissenting).

1. The Law Is a Human Creation, and Therefore It Is a Historical Phenomenon

This is, of course, a restatement of Holmes's great dictum about the life of the law. The law, at least the law as American lawyers usually discuss it, is not a transcendent set of norms floating above the human historical and political world. Instead, it is shaped (as Holmes went on to say in 1880) by "the felt necessities of the time, the prevalent moral and political theories, intuitions of public policy, avowed or unconscious." The great doctrinal systems of the late nineteenth and early twentieth centuries were not immutable principles inscribed somehow into the very nature of LAW itself; most of their substance had in fact been made up by lawyers and judges over the course of the nineteenth century and reflected the conflicts of the day and the commitments and even, Holmes added, "the prejudices judges share with their fellow men." What some people make up, other people can modify or undo... and so the law will change, as the political and moral commitments of those in positions to make decisions change. Holmes was sympathetic, up to a point, with the impulse to deny this fact: "the logical method and form flatter that longing for certainty and for repose which is in every human mind. But certainty generally is illusion, and repose is not the destiny of man." Modern American legal thought acknowledges the unavoidable reality that the legal system is never at rest, and that the law, being a form of human social thought, can never achieve certainty or unchanging consensus.[9]

The law of statutory construction provides a recent and important example of this truth. For most of the twentieth century, the dominant mode of statutory construction in American courts included a broad range of considerations, not just textual meaning but the legislature's perceived purpose and (in particular) the legislative history of the statute. It was not uncommon for a court to reject "reliance upon a literal construction" of the statute's language because of what the US Supreme Court once called the "'familiar rule that a thing may be within the letter of the statute and yet not within the statute, because not within its spirit nor within the intention of its makers.'" "When the plain meaning" of the legislature's words would produce an outcome "at variance with the policy of the legislation" *as the court perceived that policy*, the court

9. *The Common Law* in *The Essential Holmes* 237; The Path of the Law in *id.* at 167.

would "frequently . . . follow that purpose, rather than the literal words," particularly when the statute's literal meaning was inconsistent with the court's reading of the legislative history.[10]

This began to change in the 1980s, as an increasing number of judicial and academic critics led by Antonin Scalia (a US Supreme Court justice from 1986), insisted that since the words of a statute *are* the law and the only explanation of its purposes that the legislature has formally adopted, statutory construction is limited to a search for the meaning of those words. "Judges interpret laws rather than reconstruct legislators' intentions. Where the language of those laws is clear, we are not free to replace it with an unenacted legislative intent."[11] The proponents of this textualist revolution in the interpretation of statutes sometimes disagreed with one another about the extent to which textualism precludes resort to other tools besides textual argument—Justice Scalia was particularly and unusually insistent that legislative history should play no role whatever. But the textualists' success is undeniable: judicial discussion of statutory construction issues in the 2020s proceeds very differently than it typically did in the 1970s. Over that half century, the law of statutory construction changed, very significantly, in federal and most state courts.[12]

It is possible, though by no means certain, that a similar revolution in legal method is occurring in federal constitutional law. In reaction to a perceived lack of discipline and professionalism in many US Supreme Court constitutional decisions in the 1960s and 70s, some lawyers and

---

10. *United Steelworkers of Am., AFL-CIO-CLC v. Weber*, 443 U.S. 193, 201 (1979) (quoting *Holy Trinity Church v. United States*, 143 U.S. 457, 459 (1892)); *Perry v. Com. Loan Co.*, 383 U.S. 392, 400 (1966) (cleaned up). On the tendency to privilege legislative history over a "literal reading" of the statute, *see, e.g.*, *Idaho Sheet Metal Works, Inc. v. Wirtz*, 383 U.S. 190, 200 (1966) ("such a reading would attribute to Congress a purpose going well beyond its reiterated explanation . . . in [t]he legislative history").

11. *I.N.S. v. Cardoza-Fonseca*, 480 U.S. 421, 453 (1987) (Scalia, J., concurring in the judgment).

12. Justice Elena Kagan once said that "Justice Scalia has taught everybody how to do statutory interpretation differently, and I really do mean pretty much taught everybody. You know there's that classic phrase that we're all realists now. Well I think we're all textualists now in a way that just was not remotely true when Justice Scalia joined the bench." Kagan, 2015 Scalia Lecture: A Dialogue with Justice Elena Kagan on the Reading of Statutes (Harvard Law School), quoted in Stuart M. Benjamin & Kristen M. Renberg, *The Paradoxical Impact of Scalia's Campaign Against Legislative History*, 105 Cornell L. Rev. 1023, 1024 (2020).

judges began pressing the view that the only legitimate constitutional law arguments are those that rest on the meaning of the particular constitutional provision at issue as understood when it was adopted. "Originalism," as this view came to be called, found a serious adherent on the Supreme Court with the appointment of Justice Scalia, and by 2010 Justice Elena Kagan could state during her Senate confirmation hearings that in constitutional law, "we apply what [the founders] say, what they meant to do. So in that sense, we are all originalists." It is unclear that the consensus acceptance of originalism Kagan invoked is much more than rhetorical, and it remains to be seen whether a methodologically rigorous originalism will actually come to dominate federal constitutional adjudication. But there is no doubt that original-meaning arguments take up far more space in briefs and judicial opinions, and are often more sophisticated, than once was generally true.[13]

2. Judges Make Law

Dean Langdell had a simple answer to Robert Rantoul's accusation that the common law is anti-democratic. What courts do in announcing and applying the law, Langdell insisted, is entirely distinct from what legislators do when they make law. For Holmes this was obviously wrong, and its error ought to be self-evident to anyone who understands that the life of the law has been experience, that the history of English and American law is one long story of revered judges remaking the law they inherited to meet the felt necessities of the time, and doing so (this is the rub) as the judges perceived those necessities. "I recognize without hesitation," Holmes wrote in a 1917 opinion, "that judges do and must legislate." When *Seixas v. Woods* adopted the rule of *caveat emptor* in 1804, the court wasn't discovering a previously unknown fact about the universe, it was deciding between competing conceptions of when society ought to provide a legal remedy if a sales contract goes sour. *Seixas* was announcing a common law rule, but the truth of Holmes's observa-

13. Nomination of Elena Kagan to Be an Associate Justice of the Supreme Court of the United States: Hearing Before the Senate Comm. on the Judiciary, 111th Cong. 62 (2010). I have greatly oversimplified this account of originalism, which comes in many different flavors. For additional discussion, *see* H. Jefferson Powell, *The Practice of American Constitutional Law* 13–16 (2022).

tion is not limited to common law decisions: he made the assertion I just quoted in a constitutional law case, and subsequent opinions addressing issues of statutory construction have invoked it approvingly as well.[14]

The inescapability of judicial law-making does not mean that judges ought to see themselves as free to do whatever they want, whenever they want. As a general matter, Holmes thought judges can rightly make law "only interstitially; they are confined from molar to molecular motions." At the same time, Holmes thought that "the sovereign prerogative of choice" is, at the end of the day, one aspect of the task of the judge in difficult cases, and that we would all be better off if we faced facts and admitted as much.[15]

You are no doubt aware that on this issue we have returned, as a rhetorical matter, to the Langdellian dichotomy. The charge that judges are "legislating from the bench" is a common form of public criticism, and only a foolish nominee for the US Supreme Court would quote Holmes that judges do and must legislate. But we are using Langdell's language to debate issues in Holmes's world. Let me quote an opinion by Justice Scalia, one of the most vigorous critics of illegitimate judicial lawmaking in recent history: "I am not so naive (nor do I think our forebears were) as to be unaware that judges in a real sense 'make' law. But they make it as judges make it, which is to say as though they were 'finding' it."[16] Our current disagreements start out from Holmes's insight, and concern what it is appropriate for judges to do in his (our) world.

3. The Importance of External Perspectives

Looking back, one of the most striking aspects of late nineteenth-century legal thought as Dean Langdell and others presented it is the extent to which it revolved within a closed system of legal concepts. What gave the Langdellian science of jurisprudence its power and allure was in large measure its remarkable capacity to abstract from extra-legal reality,

---

14. *Southern Pacific Co. v. Jensen*, 244 U.S. 205, 221 (1917) (Holmes, J., dissenting). *See, e.g.*, *Saxbe v. Bustos*, 419 U.S. 65, 80 (1974) (statutory construction case).

15. *Southern Pacific Co. v. Jensen*, 244 U.S. 205, 221 (1917) (Holmes, J., dissenting); Holmes, Law in Science and Science in Law (1899) in *The Essential Holmes* 198.

16. *James B. Beam Distilling Co. v. Georgia*, 501 U.S. 529, 549 (1991) (Scalia, J., concurring in the judgment).

to reduce even the most complex and untidy set of human events to a timeless, contextless juristic encounter between A and B. We may doubt the extent to which actual judges confronting real controversies actually adhered to this academic model, but its existence as an ideal was a temptation to detach legal thought from social reality. The infamous *Plessy* decision of 1896 upholding de jure racial segregation on public railroads illustrates this danger of detachment in a particularly stark fashion. The state segregation law, on its face, provided for separate but equal accommodations for white and Black Americans, with an exception for "nurses attending children of the other race." Seven justices of the Supreme Court took note of the absolute even-handedness of the words of the statute and upheld its constitutionality, over Justice John Marshall Harlan's bitter complaint that "No one would be so wanting in candor as to assert" that the law had any purpose other than to segregate away Black citizens from their white fellow citizens. (No one but my colleagues, Harlan left unsaid.)

What mattered, and all that mattered, according to the *Plessy* majority, was that under the letter of the law anything provided to A had to be provided to B as well: that said, in what sense could the law be thought to treat B unequally with A? The utter unlikelihood that the railroad cars for African Americans would actually be physically equal, the cynical neutrality of the "even-handed" exception for nurses, most centrally the fact (which Harlan repeatedly pointed out) that everyone understood that the segregation law was part of an avowed campaign to sweep away what remained of Reconstruction in the South—none of these realities mattered because none of them registered on the majority's abstract Langdellian map of legal rights and privileges.[17]

As a matter of personal taste, Holmes often found complicated fact patterns something of a bore, but even if he lapsed into abstraction himself on occasion, he thought it a critical mistake to let abstract legal concepts blind lawyers and judges to extra-legal realities. "We must think things not words, or at least we must constantly translate our words into the facts for which they stand, if we are to keep to the real and the true."[18] Langdellian legal science denied the value of any perspective but the internal perspective: Holmes insisted that a lawyer or judge who can see

17. *Plessy v. Ferguson*, 163 U.S. 537, 557 (1896) (Harlan, J., dissenting).

18. Holmes, Law in Science and Science in Law in *The Essential Holmes* 198.

only what the systems and theories of the law permit is more than half blind. The law is not about itself, but about the world: it is the translation into public rules, ultimately backed up by public force, of the goals of the political community. Insofar as we want to understand the law as effective lawyers or insightful judges, we must not lock ourselves in a windowless, airtight box made up out of precedents and True Theories. None of these means that Holmes thought members of the profession should ignore legal ideas and doctrines—"the business of a lawyer is to know the law" as a mentor once told him—but to know the law you must know more than the law, and you must let your external perspectives free you from a too-credulous acceptance of "the finality of existing legal dogma." History, obviously, was a powerful tool in this effort to escape or avoid the Langdellian box—Holmes's great 1880 lectures were devoted to proving that point—but Holmes mentioned "a more enlightened understanding of economic facts" just as often.[19]

The twenty-first century law school is, through and through, a monument to Holmes in this regard. True, the courses listed in the 1L curriculum have Langdellian names, most of them, but they are taught by professors all of whom absorbed Holmes's mindset in the cradle. The upper-year curriculum and much of the scholarship published by law professors demonstrate the importance of external perspectives to contemporary legal thought in the opportunities they provide to view law with the tools not just of history and economics, but of psychology and anthropology and business and social criticism and philosophy.

4. The Importance of Self-Awareness and Restraint in the Exercise of Power

Let's return to the *Plessy* case for a moment, and recall the Langdellian abstraction that made possible the opinion of the Court with its reduction of the case to 1 = 1 therefore A = B. One might say that all this tells us is that people of ill will can use Langdellian language to cloak their evil, in this case racist, or at least brutally indifferent, motivations. Obviously so, but Holmes thought the problem goes deeper. The more self-enclosed and dogmatic a system of legal thought, the more insistent

19. The Law (1885) in *id.* at 223; Letter to Franklin Ford (Feb. 8, 1808) in *id.* at 200.

its adherents are that the law is or can be insulated from politics and social change, the more the judges believe in the goal of complete objectivity and (doubtless) their own success in achieving that goal—what these principles of Langdellian legal science add up to is a recipe for self-delusion. The judge who is utterly convinced in a hard case that he is simply following the LAW without any admixture of personal preference and emotion, and that anyone who disagrees (including his colleagues) is a knave or a fool, is almost certain, Holmes thought, to be in the grip of his own unacknowledged biases.

It may be, for all I know, that the majority justices in *Plessy* were as sure of the purity of their motives as of the logic of their reasoning. We are, all of us, prone to think that what seems obvious to us must be, by that very token, true. But as Holmes wrote, "Certitude is not the test of certainty."[20] As a scholar, Holmes urged lawyers and law students to search for the social consequences and psychological sources of our felt commitments. As a judge, Holmes both preached and practiced a commitment to restraint in the exercise of judicial power since judges are no more exempt than anyone else from contestable "moral and political theories, intuitions of public policy, avowed or unconscious, even . . . prejudices." "It is a misfortune if a judge reads his conscious or unconscious sympathy with one side or the other into the law, and forgets that what seem to him to be first principles are believed by half his fellow[s] to be wrong," Holmes remarked in a 1913 speech: "when twenty years ago a vague terror went over the earth and the word socialism began to be heard, I thought and still think that fear was translated into doctrines that had no proper place in the Constitution or the common law."[21] Precisely because judges must sometimes exercise the sovereign prerogative of choice and make law, judges ought to be slow in doing so, and when they do, they ought to understand and acknowledge that they are making choices in the exercise of power, not simply serving as the oracular voice of a brooding omnipresence in the sky.

The theme of judicial restraint runs throughout contemporary American legal thought, not just in constitutional law, where we are most apt to use the term, but in our conflicting views on statutory construction, the role of economic analysis, and the relative roles of courts and regu-

20. Natural Law (1918) in *id.* at 181.

21. *The Common Law* in *id.* at 237; Law and the Court (1913) in *id.* at 147.

latory agencies, to name only a few examples. You and I are not judges, of course, though some of you may be some day: what does this Holmesian theme have to say to us now? I have a twofold answer. Holmes was perhaps the first prominent figure in American law to emphasize the extent to which our legal convictions and conclusions are shaped by extra-legal commitments and influenced by motivated reasoning and other constraints on our thinking. We are likely to think more clearly and argue more persuasively in the law if we keep in mind the possibility that we are wrong, or at least that those who disagree with us are not, by that token alone, stupid or evil.

Nor is this merely a question of good manners, important as those are. Holmes once wrote that in our society, "there is enough community for us to talk, not enough for anyone to command."[22] His point was not that government cannot impose obligations, but rather that the community of thought, including the community of legal thought, is constituted by its commitment to dialogue and debate even among those who fundamentally disagree. Someone once described "the lawyers' contribution to the civilizing of humanity [as their] capacity to argue furiously in the court-room [or the classroom, let me add], then sit down as friends over a drink or dinner. This habit is often interpreted by the nonlawyer as a mark of their corruption [but] it is a characteristic of humane tolerance that is most desperately needed at the present time."[23] Or any time.

5. Most Questions in Law Involve Differences of Degree

The common law tradition has, speaking very generally, disfavored attempts to split the difference in legal outcomes. Perhaps this stems in part from the jury system: if a question once got to trial, traditionally the verdict came in one way or the other and that was that. Of course, as long as the jury had essentially uncontrolled discretion to decide cases submitted to it, the jurors could modulate the outcome in a civil action by adjusting the damages in accordance with their views of the equities: I've

22. Letter to Alice Stopford Green (Aug. 20, 1909) in *id.* at 116.

23. John R. Silber, Address at Boston University (1972), in *The Oxford Dictionary of American Legal Quotations* 273 (Fred R. Shapiro ed. 1993).

mentioned "smart money" damages intended to sting an unusually naughty defendant; on the other hand, the jury could award nominal damages: "yes, plaintiff, you're technically in the right, but you behaved abominably, so here's thruppence for your trouble." Once judges started hemming in the jury's discretion, the binary nature of jury verdicts became much sharper, and harsher, in its effects. And whatever a jury might do, that the answer to a legal question is, in the end, yes or no wasn't itself in dispute: it was an unexamined presupposition of legal thought.

Let me use as an example of this sort of either/or absolutism the Republic's first great constitutional controversy: whether Congress has the authority to create a national bank and, if so, what the states can do about it, if anything. In 1791, Thomas Jefferson insisted that there was no middle ground between confining Congress to the narrowest possible reading of its powers and allowing it to do whatever it wants: as he wrote to President Washington, "To take a single step beyond the boundaries thus specially drawn around the powers of Congress, is to take possession of a boundless field of power, no longer susceptible of any definition." In 1819, John Marshall turned Jefferson's reasoning upside down: the absence of any legal middle ground between a law that is absolutely necessary and one that is merely convenient meant that the Supreme Court had to accept Congress's judgment that the bank was necessary enough to satisfy the Constitution's Necessary and Proper Clause. Marshall went on to conclude that no state could tax the national bank, regardless of how small the financial imposition: "The power to tax," he wrote in *McCulloch v. Maryland*, is "the power to destroy:" if the state can demand a dollar it can demand a million dollars, and tax the bank out of existence. Jefferson and Marshall couldn't have been further apart about the bank, but they agreed completely about the yes-or-no nature of legal questions.[24]

A century after *McCulloch*, the Supreme Court decided a case called *Panhandle Oil Co. v. Knox*, which applied the *McCulloch* precedent to strike down a state tax that raised the price of gasoline for the Coast Guard. The power to tax is the power to destroy: if the state of Mississippi can impose a 3-cent-per-gallon tax that the Coast Guard ultimately

---

24. *Opinion on the Constitutionality of the Bill for Establishing a National Bank* (Feb. 15, 1791), https://founders.archives.gov/documents/Jefferson/01-19-02-0051; *McCulloch v. Maryland*, 17 U.S. (4 Wheat.) 316, 431 (1819).

must pay, Mississippi and the rest of the states can, if they choose, tax the federal government out of existence. Not so, replied Justice Holmes in dissent, the state court was right to uphold the tax.

> I should say plainly right, but for the effect of certain dicta of Chief Justice Marshall.... In those days it was not recognized as it is today that most of the distinctions of the law are distinctions of degree. If the States had any power it was assumed that they had all power, and that the necessary alternative was to deny it altogether. But this Court which so often has defeated the attempt to tax in certain ways can defeat an attempt to... go too far without wholly abolishing the power to tax. The power to tax is not the power to destroy while this Court sits.[25]

Holmes was not denying the possibility of creating hard and fast rules that are to be applied with binary, yes/no logic: indeed, he thought it useful for legislatures and courts to adopt such rules whenever possible. But even in the case of such a rule, what is usually going on, in his view, is that the rule posits polar-opposite cases, but that these opposites, when "nicely analyzed" as he put it in another opinion, exist on a spectrum. The difference between 3 cents a gallon and a million dollars a gallon is, as a practical matter, so great that we tend to think of it as a difference in kind: the million-dollar tax is a prohibition on the purchase of gas stated as if it were a tax. But in reality both amounts exist on a spectrum of burdensomeness running from minimal to prohibitive. What about a hundred dollars a gallon? One dollar? Ten cents? At some point, as we move up or down the spectrum, our evaluation of the impact *in fact* of the tax will change. Jefferson and Marshall knew that of course, but they didn't think that courts can properly draw such distinctions. Holmes did, and in this as in other matters, we are the children of Holmes.

We are thinking in Holmes's legal universe when we discuss comparative negligence in tort law (you are responsible financially for your share of the damage), or the Restatement of Contracts rule about promissory estoppel (the promisor should be held liable to the extent that justice requires), or the question of when the government must pay

25. *Panhandle Oil Co. v. Mississippi ex rel. Knox*, 277 U.S. 218, 223 (1928) (Holmes, J., dissenting).

compensation for regulating private property (basically, when the regulation goes too far in diminishing the value of the property).[26]

6. Most Questions in Law Involve Conflict between Competing and Legitimate Interests

But wait just a minute, I hear Jefferson and Marshall objecting, in agreement for once. This sort of line drawing is unsuitable for judges because there is a degree of arbitrariness in it: at some point on the spectrum the court may be compelled to hold that ninety-nine cents is okay but a dollar isn't. A legislator can pick and choose in this way, but a court can't, or shouldn't. You already know Holmes's answer to that: the sovereign prerogative of choice is part of the judicial office; judges can and must make law.

Jefferson and Marshall are tough, though, and they have one more objection. The claim that legal issues are usually questions of degree misses the very point of law, which is to distinguish the lawful from the unlawful, the legally right from the legally wrong. Either it is correct that the Constitution permits the state to tax the Coast Guard, or it doesn't. Yes or no. There is no middle ground. To which Holmes answers that the law is not a system of absolute norms on all issues; it is, much of the time, a bundle of compromises between competing interests, desires, and principles most or sometimes all of which are legitimate and none of which, perhaps, ought to be wholly sacrificed. It costs the state money to provide roads and waterways for the Coast Guard to use and police officers to see that the roads and waterways are used safely: the interest in collecting a tax to defray those costs is legitimate, but it is equally legitimate that the federal government should be able to operate the Coast Guard (and its vehicles) as economically as possible. Neither interest is illegitimate and, if possible, the law should not treat either as valueless.

> All rights tend to declare themselves absolute to their logical extreme. Yet all in fact are limited by the neighborhood of

26. *See Pennsylvania Coal Co. v. Mahon*, 260 U.S. 393, 415 (1922) (Holmes, J., for the Court).

> principles of policy which [conflict], and which become strong enough to hold their own when a certain point is reached.

Line drawing of the sort Jefferson and Marshall thought alien to judicially declared law is in reality inescapable, Holmes thought, not just because legal distinctions are matters of degree but also because at any given time the law reflects both "the pressure of the past and the conflicting wills of the present."[27]

Twenty-first century lawyers bitterly disagree not just over how to resolve particular conflicts between social interests, but also over the extent to which judges should think for themselves in terms of balancing those interests rather than seek to apply the balance struck by someone else. We do not, however, argue as if the law could ever stand above such conflicts.

Legal Realism

Someone once labeled the twentieth century the Age of Anxiety in American legal history.[28] Whatever others mean by that, the phrase captures the feeling I sometimes have that modern American law is too unstable, too fluid, too relative to whatever viewpoint I'm asked to take. The result can be a kind of intellectual vertigo, which isn't pleasant even if Holmes was right and repose is not our destiny. There is a cure for this, I think, but before I write out the prescription, we should consider one of the historical causes of the discomfort, the curious and ill-defined idea called American Legal Realism.

If you are a law student, the odds are long that you have already encountered the term Legal Realism. You may have even used it yourself, perhaps in a sentence like "that's a Legal Realist position" which can be said either as praise or disparagement. The term came into use among American lawyers shortly after 1930 to describe some themes and tendencies in the thinking and scholarship of a relatively small group of law professors; it was quickly applied, loosely and retroactively, to Holmes and Cardozo. To the extent that Legal Realism was a discrete movement

---

27. *Hudson County Water Co. v. McCarter*, 209 U.S. 349, 355 (1908) (Holmes, J., for the Court); Twenty Years in Retrospect (1902) in *The Essential Holmes* 151.

28. Professor Gilmore in *The Ages of American Law.*

in legal thought, it quickly dissipated, and we shall not consider its history. But Legal Realism as an element in the modern American legal consciousness, derived in substantial measure from figures such Holmes and Cardozo but with its own distinctive flavor, is worth a few minutes of our attention. I'm going to try to state, briefly, the central ideas that I think the term suggests, but don't take my list as a definition: Legal Realism is as much a mood as a theory or set of ideas.

(1) The law in action is not identical to the formal legal rules. The posted speed limit on the roads that I drive on in going to work is, for much of the time, 55. It would be Legal Realist observation to say that on those parts of the road, the "real" speed limit is about 61, or maybe 64: it's very unlikely that a police officer will stop you as long as you stay below this "real" legal rule, whatever the sign may say.

(2) The real explanation for a judicial decision can't be read off the face of the opinion of the court. The opinion states the judge's view of how best to justify the outcome, not why or how she got to the outcome. In reality, the judge's gut sense (her "hunch") about the best outcome in a case precedes her consultation of the formal legal authorities, and her hunches are going to reflect her individual personality, background, education, politics, and so on. The silly version of this, espoused in fact by none of the original Legal Realists, is that how the case comes out depends on what the judge had for breakfast. Less whimsically, as Cardozo said in 1920, we can see with no one's eyes but our own, and how we see a case, at least at first, will reflect that truth.

(3) In any debatable case, there are plausible legal justifications for differing outcomes. Outside criminal law, where a convicted defendant has no incentive not to appeal even a hopeless case, this means that there are at least superficially plausible arguments for both parties in any appellate case. For Dean Langdell, law was fixed, determinate, Newtonian; for Legal Realism, the law is quantum mechanics, and the uncertainty principle reigns.

There are at least three possible responses to these ideas. The first is simple denial, the attempt to return to the safety and certainty of the Langdellian universe. I think it's too late in the day for that. Justice Antonin Scalia once wrote, with his characteristic wit, that he "never thought Oliver Wendell Holmes and the legal realists did us a favor by pointing out [all this]. Those judges wise enough to be trusted with the secret already knew it."[29] Perhaps Justice Scalia was being ironic, but in any event, the cat is out of the bag. Wise or not, we're all in on the secret.

Another response to Legal Realism is to throw up one's hands and conclude that if nothing is certain, everything is up for grabs. For practicing lawyers and judges, this leads to either cynicism or despair. When you are in law school, it produces a totally understandable sense of intense frustration: what am I supposed to be learning if the rules aren't really the rules, the opinions aren't really explanations, and you can always come to any conclusion you want? No wonder modern lawyers live in the Age of Anxiety. I don't think this is the right response either, not just because I prefer my sanity, but because I think it stems from a misunderstanding of what Legal Realism actually entails.

I come then to a third response to Legal Realism, which is by the way also my promised cure for the anxiety and frustration Legal Realism can induce. The central and enduring value of Legal Realism lies in its insistence that we not lose sight of the external perspective. We fool ourselves if we treat the law as a hermetically sealed box of eternal truths, and we go astray if we think we can learn the law as a set of abstract concepts. The law is a *practice*, an activity, and thus it shapes the lawyer and the lawyer's perceptions of the world, but it is mistake to let the law become all-consuming. The law's significance lies in its impact on the world outside the law: on the speed that motorists actually drive, on the officer's decision about when to issue a citation, on the judge's hunch about the right outcome of the case. We don't understand the law itself, and cannot do our jobs as lawyers well, if we lose sight of this, if we let ourselves get trapped in a web of words detached from the things to which the words relate.

This doesn't mean that everything is up for grabs. The Legal Realist insight that the "real" speed limit on the highway is 64 doesn't mean there is no significance to that sign reading 55—change the sign to 65 and I guarantee that you'll see a change in the behavior of drivers and officers alike. The role of personality and all the rest in the way that judges and others make legal decisions doesn't mean that legal thought is a charade: for one thing the judge's hunch as to the right outcome in a case is deeply shaped by his or her training as a lawyer, a training that

29. Antonin Scalia, *Assorted Canards of Contemporary Legal Analysis*, 40 Case W. Res. L. Rev. 581, 589 (1990).

started in the fall of the future judge's 1L year. And as for there being plausible but conflicting arguments... if you put aside uncertainty about the facts, in the vast majority of cases, real and imagined, which is the better argument is usually clear, and ninety-five out of a hundred competent lawyers would agree on which argument it is. In your 1L courses you study, for the most part, appellate cases—in other words, the decisions you're reading come from the small minority about which there was room for genuine debate. You read cases that show the strength of the arguments and interests on either side of an issue not because the question wasn't resolved—at any given point in time it probably has an answer—but in order that you can understand the existing rule, its limitations, and its weaknesses.

As we saw in the first chapter, people sometimes use the term "common law" to mean a transcendent body of law, detached from the actual decisions of particular courts. The negative insight of Legal Realism is that we should give up looking for law in that sense. But none of Legal Realism's themes are at all inconsistent with another of the meanings I gave you: "common law" as a professional culture, a shared tradition about how to think about, argue over, and decide legal issues. The greatest of the figures associated with Legal Realism as a historical phenomenon was the commercial law scholar Karl Llewellyn. In 1960, long after Legal Realism as an episode was over, Llewellyn published a book entitled *The Common Law Tradition*. In the introduction, he explained that his object was to address the "corrosiveness" of the worry whether everything is in fact up for grabs in the law, whether there is "any real stability of footing for the lawyer, be it in litigation or in counseling, whether therefore there is any effective craftsmanship for him to bear to serve his client and justify his being." Or, as we might add, whether there is any there there for you to learn or me to teach in law school. Professor Llewellyn's answer was that such worries are rooted in a misunderstanding of what the law is and should be. If "law students assume that if the outcome of an appeal is not foredoomed in logic it *therefore* is the product of uncontrolled will which is as good as wayward," then it is clear that "our machinery for communicating the facts of life" about the law have gone haywire.[30]

30. Karl N. Llewellyn, *The Common Law Tradition: Deciding Appeals* 1, 4 (1960).

In reality, this prototypical Legal Realist continued, law in the United States, on the appellate-court level, is what he liked to call "reckonable," the opposite of up for grabs: "reckonable far beyond what any sane person has any business expecting from machinery devoted to settling disputes self-selected for their toughness."[31] According to Llewellyn, the law that you are studying and I try to teach, the law that gives meaning and coherence to the work of practitioners and judges, exists centrally in what he called the common law tradition, which I have described as the shared intellectual culture of the profession. Llewellyn deeply valued the external perspective on the law, and co-authored a classic book in law and anthropology, but he did not think the internal perspective of the lawyer unimportant or empty. Quite the opposite. When we understand, rightly, the internal perspective as a shared form of thought, then we know what to look for in law school and from our legal institutions.

★ ★ ★

I want to conclude this chapter by considering the distinction between the internal and external perspectives on the law, and how we might make use of them both. There are many external perspectives that you will encounter in law school and during a career as a lawyer, but how do any of them relate to the internal perspective of the lawyer's professional culture?

Let's work with a simple hypothetical case. Here are the undisputed facts: in the wake of a devastating hurricane, the state government mobilized the National Guard to provide security in the plaintiff's coastal hometown, and for the three days that the Guard was patrolling, the state authorities required the plaintiff, over his protests, to allow a squad of the Guard to sleep over in his basement. The plaintiff's claim is that he is entitled to damages for this intrusion because it was a violation of the Third Amendment to the United States Constitution: "No Soldier shall, in time of peace be quartered in any house, without the consent of the Owner, nor in time of war, but in a manner to be prescribed by law." In its response, the state's lawyers argued, correctly, that the US Supreme Court has never held that the Third Amendment applies to state governments: the district court dismissed the plaintiff's action on this ground,

31. *Id.* at 4.

and the court of appeals affirmed. The Supreme Court has agreed to hear the case: the only question before the justices is whether the Third Amendment governs actions by a state government such as that which the plaintiff alleges.

Now imagine two lawyers discussing how the Supreme Court will rule in this case, not arguing the case on behalf of a client but simply trying to predict the outcome. Stephen points out that the Court has stated more than once that whether a provision of the Bill of Rights applies to state government depends on whether the right it protects is "fundamental to our scheme of ordered liberty" as shown by the Anglo-American legal tradition.[32] The roots of the Third Amendment, in his view, lie in the English fear of standing royal armies, which the amendment brought forward into the American context by prohibiting the quartering of federal soldiers in private homes. The right the Third Amendment protects thus is intended to prevent central-government tyranny and has nothing to do with the relationship between private citizens and state employees acting as local police, and the Court will say as much.

In response, Matilda protests that under an opinion of the Court written by the great Justice Cardozo long ago, the question ought to be whether the Third Amendment protects a right that is "implicit in the concept of ordered liberty." A Bill of Rights provision like the Third Amendment applies to state government if, in Cardozo's words, "neither liberty nor justice would exist if [the right] were sacrificed." Surely, she argues, being coerced into allowing armed and unwelcome guests into one's home is a serious affront to liberty, and denying the plaintiff damages for the intrusion is a sacrifice of justice itself. This, Matilda insists, is the better argument, and the Court will see as much.[33]

And so their conversation might take off. I picture Stephen and Matilda going on to a close reading of Supreme Court opinions, debating the role of precedent, arguing about English history and the status of the National Guard, worrying over the consequences of a decision one way or the other, and bringing their own moral and political convictions

32. *Timbs v. Indiana*, 139 S. Ct. 682, 687 (2019). *See id.* at 687 (discussing Magna Carta, the English Bill of Rights, the Virginia Declaration of Rights, and post-Revolutionary era state constitutions).

33. *Palko v. State of Connecticut*, 302 U.S. 319, 326 (1937).

to bear on the correct way to answer the question before the Court. Whatever their ultimate prediction about the Court's decision, they are talking from within the internal, lawyer's perspective, and we should expect to find much the same debate in the briefs and arguments before the Court, within the justices' chambers, and laid out in the opinion of the Court when the Court actually answers the question.

But now imagine a rather different conversation. Matilda, let us say, begins in the same way, worrying over legal concepts such as "ordered liberty" and how they should be used in deciding whether the Third Amendment applies to state governments. This time, however, Stephen interrupts: "You're missing the point. The Supreme Court's decisions are entirely determined by economic considerations, and in particular by the interest of the justices, individually and collectively, in maximizing their power and importance. The Court will hold that the Third Amendment applies against the states, and its opinion will no doubt use the sort of rhetoric that mesmerizes you, but the reason the Court will reach this conclusion is that in doing so the justices will enhance their own power and prestige." If Stephen manages to intimidate Matilda by his self-confidence or even statistical analyses of Supreme Court decisions, this will be a conversation (or maybe I should say a monologue with witness) that is about the law but not within it. If Matilda refuses to allow Stephen to switch the conversation from the internal to the external perspective, we will end up with a shouting match.

Let me be clear, the argument I just foisted onto Stephen is a quite ridiculous caricature of any real external-perspective argument, the present-day equivalent of the silly "did the judge eat eggs for breakfast" version of Legal Realism. But the fundamental mistake in the second conversation we imagined is that Matilda and Stephen were talking at cross purposes. Any sophisticated modern lawyer will want to know as much as he can about what the courts are likely to do in a case he has to brief or argue, but statistical studies about judicial behavior won't write his brief: you can't tell the Court that a reason for ruling for my client is that the political scientists predict that you will do so. Still less will the statistical studies help the judge decide what she *ought* to decide; for that she will need the internal perspective. The internal perspective on the law is intrinsically normative; the external perspectives, all of them, are descriptive from the standpoint of the law. To be a fully rounded lawyer, you need both, but the heart of legal education, and above all the central objective of your first year in law school, is to enter into the culture and tradition of the law, to learn for yourself the internal perspective.

Modern American legal thought begins with Holmes's insistence that "We must constantly translate our words into the facts for which they stand if we are to keep to the real and the true." But that doesn't make the language of the law empty or unimportant. A great twentieth-century lawyer, Charles Alan Wright, once wrote that "The only tool of the lawyer is words.... Whether we are trying a case, writing a brief, drafting a contract, or negotiating with an adversary, words are the only things we have to work with." As lawyers, we keep to the real and the true through words.[34]

34. Wright, Book Review, Townes Hall Notes (1988) at 5.

FIVE

Lawtalk 101: The Language and Arguments of Contemporary American Law

In his classic account of the first year in law school, Scott Turow tells us that after a couple of weeks, he and his classmates "were beginning to inject [a] new vocabulary into their conversation, speaking Legal to each other. People were self-conscious about how oratorical and windy they sounded... but most of us persisted, practicing on each other." Turow's civil procedure professor "neatly summed up what we were all trying to do in using legalisms."

> In the last meeting of Civil Procedure that week, a woman answered a question [the professor] had posed. "The court does not have subject matter jurisdiction over the person," she said.
>
> "I'm not sure I know what that means, [he replied], but I'm still glad to hear you talk that way. After all," he said, "you can't be a duck until you learn to quack."[1]

If Turow's professor actually made the crack about the duck, he was being a bit too cute: learning lawtalk is not a matter of memorizing strange terms or injecting them into your conversation. But taken at a less superficial level, what Turow is describing is the heart of the first-

1. Scott Turow, *One L* 60–61 (1977). Turow wrote *One L* while he was still in law school, and went on to become not only a successful attorney but also a best-selling author, many of whose novels involve lawyers and courtroom battles.

year experience: the student's immersion in the words, the ways of thinking and arguing, the mindset, that characterize what I've called the professional culture of American law. In this chapter, we're going to look at some specific aspects of contemporary legal language and thought. Law students quickly meet much of what I have to say in the fall of your 1L year; I think that it will be useful, nonetheless, to draw out these themes and briefly study them apart from the ways they come up in classes on torts or property or legal research and writing.

Lawtalk Is an Artificial Language; Legal Concepts Are the Tools of a Specific Craft

This first point is, in my judgment, absolutely crucial. Even if it is already obvious to you, it is worth a few minutes to point out its significance. Remember Sir Edward Coke telling James I that the king couldn't decide legal cases himself because doing so "requires long Study and Experience" in "the artificial Reason of the Law?" James, a man of considerable learning who had written two books on political theory, thought himself as competent as any lawyer to figure out what is the just and reasonable way to resolve a controversy. Coke's answer—and it is the answer of twenty-first century American law as well—is that within the legal system controversies are resolved through the language and thought-ways of the law. That language, those ways of thinking, the modes of argument they permit and require, are simply not identical to the sort of reasoning people (including lawyers) employ in making other kinds of decisions, although there is of course an overlap. Lawtalk and legal reasoning are (to use Coke's term) "artificial," constructed for a specific purpose, and you need to understand this artificial language if you are to function within the legal system.

Coke's point wasn't merely that King James wouldn't be *as good* a judge as Lord Coke because he lacked Coke's training, so that for example James would be less able to decide correctly to whom Blackacre belonged because he was unfamiliar with the details of English property law. King James couldn't be a judge *at all*, at least not in a court of common law, because the use of specifically legal concepts and modes of reasoning and argument as the tools of thought and decision are what distinguish the law from other human practices. What counts as a legal argument—as opposed to a moral, religious, economic, or political one—is the principal component in determining just what law is. This is why lawyers often argue so fiercely over what might seem like mere rules of debate, over (for example) whether you are allowed to cite efficiency arguments in construing a statute or foreign law in determining what is a "cruel and unusual punishment" under the US Constitution. What counts as law and what it is to do law are determined by the words, ideas, and arguments we accept as legitimate within the legal system. And, crucially, the "we" that is relevant here is the legal profession, not (or not directly) the political system more generally or American society as a whole.

Let's see what this means concretely. For simplicity's sake I'll write in terms of lawtalk in litigation, but the point is equally true in situations where lawyers play a different role. When lawyers talk about the human events that have led, or might lead, to a legal controversy, they use concepts that derive their meaning from the law, not, primarily, from the events that took place in the extra-legal world. In fact, it doesn't go too far, I think, to say that legal concepts are entirely artificial. You don't find torts or contracts or even property out there in the universe. Things exist and events happen in the physical and human and social world that result, or may result, in controversies. Someone gets careless and as a result someone else gets hurt. Two people make a deal and one of them backs out. I start holding regular loud parties in my basement and you can't get any sleep. Lawyers will talk about the commission of a tort, or ask whether there was a contract, or debate whether my parties are a nuisance, but "tort" and "contract" and "nuisance" are terms of art. Whether one of them applies to something that happened in the human world is, in the end, a question of whether the extra-legal events fit into the legal category, and that in turn depends on the goals and policies that the law embodies and seeks to advance. This can be confusing since some lawyer words are used by non-lawyers as well: before I went to law school, I thought I knew what a "contract" was—a piece of paper you have to sign in some situations—and that "nuisances" were things like forgetting your umbrella when it's going to rain. Beginning in my 1L year, I learned that lawyers use these and other words differently.

As lawtalk, concepts such as contract and nuisance and tort serve to structure legal analysis, to separate promises that the law will "enforce," parties the law should shut down, careless acts that should lead to an award of money "damages," from events in the human world that may look very similar. The differences between two promises or parties or accidents may be minuscule or even non-existent from many perspectives, but for some reason of principle or policy legal decisionmakers have decided to treat them differently: contract and nuisance and tort—those artificial legal constructs—are the tools by which legal advisors counsel and litigators argue and judges determine where the lines of legal difference lie. And it is lawtalk and legal reasoning that define as well what it means to "enforce" a promise and how "damages" are calculated.

Since legal concepts are artificial tools that lawyers use instrumentally and normatively rather than value-free attempts to describe the world neutrally, how a particular concept maps onto the extra-legal universe is often debatable. Take a simple example. As you're driving down the road at dusk you see me walking on your side, and in the roadway: to make sure I know you're coming, you politely toot your horn. Unfortunately, Stephen, who's in his car coming the other way, is startled by your toot and runs into the ditch, in the process knocking over Matilda's mailbox. No one got hurt, but Matilda needs her mailbox fixed. Who caused the accident? Me? You? Stephen? The right answer, if we're talking about events in the physical world, might be all three of us, not to mention the thief who stole my car which meant I had to walk home in the first place. But who, if anyone, has to pay for Matilda's broken mailbox? We can't answer that legal question simply by deciding whether, as a matter of physics or human behavior, it makes sense to call me or you or Stephen a cause; the legal answer may well depend on how we apply the legal concept of "proximate cause."

When I was first studying tort law it made sense to me that the defendant is liable only if he or she was the "proximate" cause of the accident, but I was mystified to read that the "concept of proximate cause... stems from policy considerations."[2] What that means, I eventually discovered, is that in tort law the word "proximate" isn't simply a fancy synonym for a word such as "immediate" in an ordinary, what happened in the world, sense. Instead, "proximate cause" is an artificial concept by which some common-law legal system distinguishes defendants who ought to be financially responsible from those who, for whatever reasons of fairness

---

2. *Derdiarian v. Felix Contracting Corp.*, 51 N.Y.2d 308, 314 (1980).

or policy, should not. Someone may be, in a very real sense, a cause of the accident (lawyers sometimes say a "but-for cause") and yet not be the *proximate* cause because the legal system has concluded that it would unjust or inefficient to make someone in that person's circumstances financially responsible for the accident. Much of legal argument consists of debating whether some legal concept of this sort ought to be applied to what we understand happened in the extra-legal world.

For Most Purposes in the Law, Arguments Must Always Be Translated into Lawtalk

We start with events or interests or things in the world beyond law, but to bring the law to bear on them we must translate all our arguments into the language of the law. I've quoted Holmes advising us to keep translating our words into the things for which they stand, but the opposite is true as well. The lawyer listening to a client describing his interests or his problems starts with what may be, even on the part of a very sophisticated business client, a confusing mass of information and intentions that don't fit any obvious legal category: much of the lawyer's job will be to figure out how the concepts of the law best map onto the facts and the client's needs. A lawyer giving advice or helping structure a deal must then determine how to advance the client's interests in ways that the legal system will recognize as legitimate. In presenting a case to a jury, or trial judge, or appellate court, the litigator is trying to persuade the decisionmaker that what happened in the human and social world is best described in the terms of one legal concept or another. And it is the job of the judge to choose and apply those concepts to achieve the purposes of the legal system, which sometimes do not coincide very closely with the interests or goals of any of the parties.

What this means is that just as the medieval forms of action served to channel some disputes into royal court and before a jury, while pushing other controversies elsewhere, twenty-first century lawtalk acts as a gatekeeper for non-lawyers' claims. Lawtalk is not only a tool that lawyers use, it is also, most of the time, the exclusive tool that they must ultimately use. The non-lawyers we advise and represent usually don't care about the meaning of proximate cause or any other legal concept—what concerns them are the stakes for them in the extra-legal world. Therefore, as Holmes cautioned, we must constantly be thinking about the world beyond the law rather than in legal abstractions.

But you and I can serve the client's interests—and in the end the goals of the legal system itself—only by translating those interests into the terms and concepts used within the legal system. The task of constant translation runs both ways. Telling a court that "it just wouldn't be fair" if the defendant didn't pay for that broken mailbox doesn't work: simple fairness may well be the heart of our case, but we need to find a way to translate that perhaps convincing human intuition into lawtalk. Lawyering involves the constant attempt to relate what we are trying to accomplish in the extra-legal universe to the language of the law.

Legal Thought Is a Form of Authority-Based Reasoning

Lawtalk is an artificial language, and legal reasoning is doubly artificial. Lawyers and judges address problems in the human social world using the law's unique terms and concepts rather than the language others would employ, *and* the decisions they reach are not necessarily what the individual lawyer personally would conclude is the right legal answer in the abstract. They are instead what he or she thinks is the conclusion demanded by the relevant authority. Legal reasoning is therefore quite distinct from the sort of thinking we employ, if we're wise, in extra-legal situations.

In many areas of personal and social life, if we want someone to decide X, it makes sense to argue that all things considered, X is the best decision. If you're trying to argue me into adopting the so-called Mediterranean diet, you might look up information on the internet about it being heart-healthy, good for my waistline, better for the planet, and so on—in other words you might try to persuade me to agree with you that it would be better, all things considered, if I decided to switch to the Mediterranean diet, and in doing so you might employ what you knew of dieticians' and doctors' technical vocabularies. On the other hand, you might just tell me to eat Mediterranean because Uncle Clifton always said so. Not that Uncle Clifton knew anything about nutrition, and not that you yourself actually think Mediterranean is best (you're a devotee of keto) but because in our family Uncle Clifton has the final word on lifestyle choices. He is the relevant authority.

Uncle Clifton-type arguments run throughout the law. Think about the right to remain silent, familiar to all of us from the *Miranda* warning that cops in films and television are always giving people. Is it a good idea, all things considered, to allow someone who may have committed a crime to stand mute, neither helping the police in their investigation nor answering questions in open court? Don't answer too quickly: I can think of reasons going both ways. But in the United States, your right to remain silent doesn't rest on which side of the argument is more persuasive; it rests, ultimately, on the Fifth Amendment to the United States Constitution, which announces that no person "shall be compelled in any criminal case to be a witness against himself." Maybe the Fifth Amendment is a good idea, maybe it's dumb, but until the amendment is changed or repealed, the right not to incriminate oneself is a rule of law.[3]

The same is true for the requirements of the Clean Water Act, the 55 mph speed limit on those highways I've mentioned, and that ordinance the city council passed last week about clearing snow from the sidewalk within six hours of the snow stopping—all of these are legal rules not by virtue of their wisdom, all things considered, but by virtue of the fact that they were adopted (for whatever reasons) by a legal institution with the authority to make that rule. As a result, if it matters to the advice I am giving my client or the case I am arguing to the court, I can and will argue that a court or government official must follow the federal act, or the state speed limit, or the city ordinance because it is an authority, not because the judge or the official thinks it is a good idea, all things considered.

What about those *Miranda* warnings that the police have to give? The opinion of the United States Supreme Court in *Miranda v. Arizona* (1966) was an attempt to persuade the reader that the warnings were needed, in the absence of some other means of protecting the right to be silent, to prevent infringement of the Fifth Amendment right. But the existence of the right was, for the Court and everyone else, a given: in the American legal system, constitutional provisions are authorities by definition. Once decided, furthermore, the Court's *Miranda* requirements became legal authorities themselves, binding on lower courts and

3. *See Miranda v. Arizona*, 384 U.S. 436 (1966).

police officers regardless of whether those other officials are persuaded by the Court's reasoning. In the over half century since the Supreme Court decided *Miranda*, arguments over whether the warnings are a good idea, all things considered, have raged. They appear to be unending, and the Court itself has created a somewhat complicated system of exceptions, identifying situations where the warnings don't have to be given or a mistake doesn't matter, but the basic rule remains in place. As a result, in any situation where the *Miranda* rule or its exceptions are relevant, lawyers can and will argue that a court or government official must follow the Supreme Court's *Miranda* line of cases not because the Court's reasoning is persuasive, but because the Court's decisions are controlling precedents. The Supreme Court, the American legal system's Uncle Clifton, has said so.[4]

Legal thought in our professional culture is, then, a form of authority-based reasoning. Legal authorities are to be followed not because of their intrinsic merits but because of their source. They are the legal system's equivalent to "do it because Uncle Clifton said to." All sorts of interesting distinctions and perplexities follow from the central role that authority-based reasoning thus plays in our system.[5]

Let's begin with an obvious and elementary point: to count as reasoning based on authority, the authority you invoke has to be a relevant *legal* authority. I've already made the point that legal reasoning is artificial, and to serve as *legal* reasoning it must stay within the bounds of the law's peculiar and artificial language. The same can be said of legal authorities: they must be, first of all, *legal* authorities, sources of normative thought that are recognized as law in and by the American legal system. Neither the Bible, nor the *New York Times*, nor the collected works of Karl Marx or Milton Friedman, are legal authorities anywhere in the US legal system, no matter how much an individual lawyer or judge may respect any of them.

---

4. In *Dickerson v. United States*, 530 U.S. 428 (2000), the Supreme Court invalidated a statutory provision that had attempted to abrogate the *Miranda* warnings requirement in federal court cases. The Court did not revisit on the merits the much earlier *Miranda* decision's conclusion that the warnings were needed to safeguard the Fifth Amendment right; its decision to strike down the statute rested on *Miranda*'s status as precedent.

5. For more on the difference between the law's authority-based reasoning and ordinary decision making, see Frederick Schauer's outstanding book *Thinking Like a Lawyer: A New Introduction to Legal Reasoning* (2012).

Equally elementary is a second point: to be relevant legal authority, an American statute or judicial decision or other statement of law has to stem from an institution with the legitimate authority to make it law as to the question at hand. Let me explain what I mean. The Congress of the United States, the Supreme Court of the United States, and the Durham City Council all have the power to create legal authorities. On any given issue one of them may have created the legal authority that everyone else must follow on the subject. Neither Congress nor the Court, for example, has any power to rewrite the Durham, North Carolina, City Council's Unified Development Ordinance. (The state legislature could, but that's another matter involving the state's constitutional arrangements.) If the issue I am working on involves a question about off-street parking in Durham, the ordinance is probably the controlling authority.

A final point—obvious in the abstract but often tricky in practice—is that a legal authority such as a case or statute can't actually inform one's advice or structure one's brief or direct one's decision unless you understand the authority and how it applies to the issue at hand. There are at least five situations in which you and I may find ourselves unsure whether a legal authority that appears relevant on its face—whether it is a statute, regulation, judicial decision, whatever—is in fact controlling.

Problems with Using Authority

The first problem stems from ambiguity. We simply may not be certain what the case or statute or regulation means, or how it applies to our facts. The law that says I must drive at or below the posted speed limit isn't very ambiguous when the sign just reads 55, but what if the speed limit sign gives two figures: a "55" at the top of the sign and below it "trucks 45?" What counts as a truck for this purpose if no statute defines the word? Is my very small pickup a "truck" because the manufacturer called it a "truck," while your monster SUV, which is longer and weighs 50% more, isn't?

A second problem grows out of exceptions. All legal principles and rules have exceptions. I'm sure there is an exception to that one as well (besides the obvious self-contradiction), but you get the point: the existence of exceptions creates not only issues about how to understand the exceptions but also questions about how they relate to the main rule. Consider this rule: drive at or below the posted speed limit except when passing a stopped emergency vehicle, in which case you must reduce your speed, whatever it was. The exception is itself potentially ambiguous: I think it's clear that a police car with its lights flashing triggers the exception, but what about a dark police car with no officer in it or even in sight? The more complicated a legal authority is, the more the trouble its exceptions and qualifications can cause. Was the police officer supposed to read the suspect his *Miranda* rights? The answer to that question depends not just on the basic rule, but also on the many exceptions subsequent cases have created.

Justice Holmes taught us **the third source of difficulty** long ago: legal rules and principles are limited by **the existence of other rules and principles** that overlap and conflict. How do we reconcile two rules each of which seems relevant and neither of which can simply be abandoned even though they point to opposite conclusions? The law about slowing down when passing a stopped emergency vehicle isn't the only legal authority relevant to how fast I should drive: I'm also required by law as a general matter to obey directions by a police officer. What if the officer standing by her car signals to me to speed up so I get past her more quickly?

Most of constitutional law stems from this problem. With a couple of exceptions,[6] the United States Constitution does not directly regulate the activities of private persons, i.e., people who are not government officials or acting with the authority of government. The Constitution comes into play, therefore, when there is a controversy or question about some governmental action. State and local police officers ordinarily have the authority (from state or local law) to maintain order in public spaces, and that may include requiring someone to move along or otherwise act in ways the individual would rather not. But if the officer's order is based on the fact that the individual is wearing a tee shirt with the slogan "Defund the Police," we have a potential conflict with a federal rule of law,

---

6. You no doubt expected there to be exceptions! They are the Thirteenth Amendment's ban on slavery and the Twenty-First Amendment's bar on transporting liquor into a state against the state's laws (the latter regulation of private behavior is purely theoretical). Case law also establishes that in some circumstances the right of interstate travel applies to private persons interfering with someone else's right to travel.

the First Amendment to the US Constitution, which protects "freedom of speech," including printed speech on a garment.

To be sure, it is clear which authority prevails if both apply to the particular situation—as part of the Constitution, the First Amendment is "the supreme Law of the Land...any Thing in the Constitution or Laws of any State to the Contrary notwithstanding." But the Supreme Court case law applying the Free Speech Clause of the amendment includes exceptions to its general rule, some of which reflect the Court's concern to reduce the constitutional rule's interference with what the decisions view as the legitimate regulation of public property. Conflict between constitutional authorities (rules derived from the Constitution) and actions based on other legal authorities, including acts of Congress and decisions of the president, is the very definition of a constitutional controversy. And the correct resolution of the conflict does not automatically follow from the general principle that a federal constitutional authority overrides any other authority when both are legally relevant.

A fourth problem stems from the fact that not all (genuinely legal) authorities are controlling in a particular situation. American lawyers have no difficulty in recognizing that the British Defamation Act 2013 (c 26) is a genuinely *legal* authority, and the same is true for court decisions in England and Wales construing and applying it. They are not like, for example, the writings of the philosopher John Rawls, which aren't statements of law at all in the American sense. Nevertheless, neither the act of Parliament nor its judicial interpretations are controlling as to any question of American law; they are law but *foreign* law. What about California Code of Civil Procedure section 425.16, the state's anti-SLAPP law,[7] which creates a process for quickly dismissing defamation lawsuits determined to be interferences with the right of free speech? In California courts, section 425.16 is controlling authority, but it is foreign law in the courts of Hawai'i, and it would be an obvious (indeed, unimaginable) error for a Hawai'ian court to apply the provision, or treat California decisions addressing section 425.16 as controlling.

7. The acronym stands for Strategic Lawsuits Against Public Participation. As the California statute describes them, such lawsuits are "brought primarily to chill the valid exercise of the constitutional rights of freedom of speech and petition for the redress of grievances." 425.16(a). By one count, "[a]s of April 2022, 32 states and the District of Columbia [had] anti-SLAPP laws." Austin Vining & Sarah Matthews, Overview of Anti-SLAPP Laws (Reporters Committee for Freedom of the Press 2022).

All of this is no doubt obvious, but let's ask a follow-up question: are there any circumstances in which a lawyer in Hawai'i might cite, or an Hawai'ian court might invoke, the case law applying section 425.16? The answer is yes. In construing the provision, the California courts necessarily deal with legal questions the two states' legal systems share: the meaning and scope of "defamation," the existence and application of common-law defenses, and the extent to which tort liability is limited by the First Amendment. On any of those issues, a Hawai'ian court might find the reasoning of a California 425.16 decision persuasive and follow it in the absence of controlling Hawai'i authority to the contrary. And since Hawai'i has an anti-SLAPP law that is largely parallel to section 426.16, a California case might be persuasive authority even on a question about the proper construction of the Hawai'i statute's text.

What about the Defamation Act and its caselaw? Except in the unlikely case of an exact verbal parallel with a relevant American statute, there are few ways the act itself would be useful to an American court, but the same may not be true of the English/Welsh cases: the modern law of defamation in England and in the United States shares a common ancestor in the pre-Revolutionary common law, and borrowings (both ways) occasionally take place even now. It *is* possible that a judge applying the act might present a line of argument that would be persuasive to his or her American counterparts. In contrast, it is difficult to imagine a lawyer or judge citing Rawls in a brief or opinion except as a display of extralegal erudition; statements of moral and political philosophy aren't legal authorities in any sense, however persuasive they may be in their own domain.

The contrasting ideas of controlling (or binding or mandatory) authority and persuasive authority complicate the roles that legal authorities play in American lawtalk. A relevant and controlling authority cannot properly be ignored: if the statutory provision or precedent or other rule cannot be distinguished—shown to be inapplicable due to some particular aspect of the authority or of the situation under review—it must be applied. In contrast, persuasive authority vastly enlarges the well of legal arguments on which the lawyer or judge may draw without obliging anyone to do so. As Holmes taught us, there is no brooding omnipresence of general common law—or general constitutional law either—to which the states must bow: the common law of Iowa and the law derived from its constitution are as unique to the state as its body of statutes, and even exact verbal parallels do not oblige Iowa courts to follow other states' views on *their* law. But Iowa courts can look to the law of any other state as well as the decisions of the federal courts as persuasive authorities; wise judges often do in cases of legal uncertainty, and smart lawyers help them do so.

The American system of federalism further complicates the picture. The US Constitution, and constitutionally valid federal laws, treaties, and regulations, are the supreme law of the land, and both state and federal courts must apply them even if that entails ignoring a contrary state legal rule—in that circumstance, we say that the state rule is "preempted" but what we really mean is that the Supremacy Clause of Article VI of the Constitution prohibits the state rule's application. By the rule of "vertical precedent" (lower courts must follow higher courts) this means that all state and lower federal courts must treat relevant US Supreme Court decisions on any issue of federal law as controlling authority. But the lower federal courts are not superior to the state courts, and thus the decisions of the federal courts of appeals are not controlling in state courts (even states that are within the geographic jurisdiction of the particular federal appeals court), and of course state decisions on federal law do not bind federal courts.

Thus, the final judicial authority on a question of federal law—apart from the US Supreme Court—depends on which judicial system is in view: the Supreme Court of Tennessee and the US Court of Appeals for the Sixth Circuit have the final word on federal law questions in a Tennessee matter in, respectively the state courts and the federal district courts in the state.[8] When the legal question at issue is a matter of state law, the principle of vertical precedent requires all courts to acknowledge the decisions of the state's highest court as controlling authority,

8. Yes, that *does* mean that there can be two diametrically opposed views on, say, a question of federal constitutional law in the state of Tennessee, depending on which court system you're in, unless the US Supreme Court straightens out the mess. As a practical matter this deeply troubling possibility is not as common as one might fear, in large measure because a defendant in a state-court action can "remove" the case to federal district court if it involves a question of federal law or the district court would have had jurisdiction based on the citizenship of the parties.

and thus a federal court obliged to address a state law issue must base its decision on what the court thinks the state high court would hold.[9]

Earlier in this book, we discussed the uniform laws proposed by what is now known as the Uniform Law Commission, and the Restatements of the law propounded by the American Law Institute. Uniform laws are drafted by the commission as legislative proposals that a state legislature can enact as is or use as a model in drafting a statute, and courts sometimes treat the commission's comments on its proposed laws as persuasive authority in interpreting state legislation based on a uniform law. (The Hawai'i anti-SLAPP law mentioned above is a modified version of the commission's Uniform Public Expression Protection Act.) The ALI's Restatements are regularly treated as (highly) persuasive authority by many courts, and the Model Penal Code it published in 1962 sometimes receives the same treatment, although the code's major role, as its name indicates, has been to provide a model for statutory criminal law reform. Finally, treatises and other scholarly writing on law can be persuasive authority, and some such works are widely cited. However influential, however, persuasive authority remains just that—to be followed if persuasive but never mandatory.

The fifth source of difficulty over the controlling force of a legal authority depends on whether it is a rule or a principle (people sometimes say a rule or a standard). Let's unpack this distinction with a couple of examples. "Do not drive faster than the posted speed limit" is a rule: if I am driving and 55 is posted, the rule applies and is controlling: 56 mph and I am in violation of the law. Of course, a rule may be ambiguous or have exceptions or be limited by some other legal rule, but an authority that is a rule is controlling if it applies factually.

Now consider the following statute, some version of which is in force in every state: "In no circumstance shall any driver operate a motor vehicle at a speed that is reckless or unsafe." With a complication I shall note in a moment, you cannot tell whether I was conforming to this law simply by noting the speed I was going. If it is raining hard or there is ice on the road, it may be unsafe to drive at the posted limit, and I can be in

9. Yes, that *does* mean that a federal court is obliged to follow its prediction as to the state high court's views even when, for example, it is construing a state statute that is identically worded to a federal law that the US Supreme Court has authoritatively construed. There is no brooding omnipresence requiring a state supreme court to understand a given set of words in the same way those words have been understood by some other court. The state statute means what the state high court says it means.

violation of the law even though I am driving well below the speed limit. This sort of statute isn't a rule; instead, it imposes a standard or principle. The law applies to my driving, in the sense that it is controlling. But whether I was following it or violating it requires a judgment about the relation between the facts in the "real" (= extra-legal) world, and the objectives that the law embodies.

Now consider the following statute, which exists in some form in some states: "Any driver operating a motor vehicle at a speed faster than 70 miles per hour is guilty of reckless driving." The point of such a law in a state that has one is to impose the higher penalty the state ordains for reckless driving rather than the lesser penalty for mere speeding. Can I successfully beat the more expensive ticket (or worse!) by proving that although I was going 71 in a 65 mph zone, it was perfect 65-degree weather in broad daylight, and I was on a four-lane divided highway that the state's own engineers rate as factually safe at any speed below 80 under such conditions? No—remember that lawtalk is artificial. The statutory language about "reckless driving" does not directly refer to the physics, engineering, and driver reaction times that would determine an engineer or scientist's judgment about how likely it was I would have an accident. Instead, "reckless driving," in this law, means by definition "any speed over 70." The statute isn't a standard or principle but a rule, and we *can* determine whether I violated it by simply clocking my speed.

The difference between a rule and a standard (or principle) has to do with the contrasting ways each attempts to achieve its goal or objective. All legal authorities have a point: they don't just exist for their own sake. A rule attempts to achieve its objective by laying down a precise guide for behavior; a standard or principle articulates its objective and leaves room for fact-specific discretion about how to obey it on the part of those it governs, as well as room for fact-specific judgment on the part of those who must apply it. The posted speed limit rule is precise, in itself: 54 is lawful and 56 is not. The "never drive faster than is safe" principle leaves room for discretion and judgment: I have to decide when the factual circumstances require me to drive slower than 55, and the traffic court judge must decide whether my driving under those circumstances met the standard of safety that is the objective of the principle. Both rules and principles are legal authorities—they are binding because the relevant legal Uncle Clifton said so. But they bind those they govern in different ways.

How to Do Things with Statutes

I'm going to refer to statutes for the sake of simplicity, but what I have in mind are not just acts of Congress or a state legislature, but any text promulgated by an institution with the power to make law by legal instruments that are law in themselves: the articles and amendments of the Constitution of the United States, the ordinances of the City of Durham, the rules and regulations of the Federal Trade Commission, executive orders issued by the president, and so on. In all of these instances, the words of the document are themselves "the law."[10] The contrast I want you to have in mind is between statutes (and so on) and that other great set of legal authorities, judicial decisions. A judicial decision is, or contains, the law because it governs those to whom it is directed on the matters it addresses, *and* under the doctrine of *stare decisis* the decision is a precedent for later courts; the force of a precedent depends on the reasoning of the decision rather than the precise words in which that reasoning is formulated. In contrast, a statute (constitutional provision, regulation, etc.) is the law because the words it contains were made law by someone with authority to do so, and the force of the statute depends, at least in theory, on how it is worded. This is an over-simplification, as we shall see, but the basic distinction is fundamental.

Since the very language of the statute is law, that language is, in and of itself, controlling authority where it applies, and the starting point for statutory construction is the language, the exact words that it employs. Sometimes that is the ending point as well: the statute's relevance for the advice I need to give, or the brief I'm writing, or the case I'm deciding, may be clear. However, there are several reasons why it often turns out that more is needed than a quick look at the statutory text with a dictionary in hand. Poor draftsmanship is often a problem, exacerbated by the

---

10. Three quick notes: Sometimes statutory texts contain material that doesn't itself create legal rules, such as a preamble or legislative findings. Such language may be highly important in construing the provisions that *do* create rules. And legislative bodies sometimes adopt resolutions that have no formal legal effect at all, but are expressions of the legislative majority's views on some matter. Finally, the terminology used for the documents produced by legislative bodies varies, both among the various kinds of legislature (think the city council versus the Congress) and within single legislatures. A "concurrent resolution" approved by the US Senate and House of Representatives, for example, is not presented to the president for signature or veto and makes no law, while a "joint resolution" is presented and is as fully a law as a congressional "act."

convoluted processes that lie behind much modern legislation. But not even the most careful attention to detail by the most skilled legislator or regulation-drafter can avert the possibility that a law's meaning will turn out to be ambiguous in application. As James Madison put it in 1788, "all new laws, though penned with the greatest technical skill, and passed on the fullest and most mature deliberation, are considered as more or less obscure and equivocal."[11]

Furthermore, perfect clarity is very often not the actual objective of the majority that voted for the statute, especially when we are talking about statutes in the literal sense: legislation of any complexity or that has excited any controversy on its way to enactment is regularly the product of compromise between legislators whose objectives may overlap but are not identical. One way to assemble the majority necessary to pass such a bill is to use language that is deliberately vague or subject to conflicting interpretations, which leaves each of the groups that make up the majority hoping that the administrators or judges who must later apply the statute will adopt its favored interpretation.

So, let's imagine a poorly written, unavoidably ambiguous, or intentionally imprecise law. Statutory ambiguity gives judges heartburn since their job is to interpret the statute correctly—but what, after all, is the correct reading of an ambiguous text? From the standpoint of a lawyer advising or representing a client, on the other hand, statutory or regulatory ambiguity is by no means always a bad thing: after all, if the law's meaning is genuinely unclear there is space to argue that it should be read in a way that favors my client's interests! In any event, for our differing purposes we all have to make sense out of this unclear law that we're imagining. How do we do so when the words on their own fall short of clarity? Already in 1805, Chief Justice Marshall wrote that "Where the mind labours to discover the design of the legislature, it seizes every thing from which aid can be derived."[12] I want to suggest three places "from which aid can be derived."

An old source of enlightenment lies in what the common law courts have traditionally called the canons of construction—canon in the sense of measure or rule. Some of the traditional canons are indeed more or less common-sensical rules of thumb about how to read a document:

11. *The Federalist* No. 37 (J. Madison), at 236 (Jacob E. Cooke ed. 1961).

12. *United States v. Fisher*, 6 U.S. (2 Cranch) 358, 386 (1805).

general words are to be given their general meaning, the verb "to include" introduces examples rather than a complete list, every part of the statute should be given effect if possible, and so on. Other canons of construction reflect substantive commitments on the part of the courts. As mentioned earlier, the pre-modern English courts devised a canon stating that statutes in derogation of the common law are to be construed narrowly—in other words, to the extent possible a court should minimize the extent to which the legislature has imposed its choices and displaced judge-made law. Modern American courts often invoke the so-called "avoidance canon"—where fairly possible, choose an interpretation of the statute that avoids serious questions about its constitutionality. When I went to law school, most of the canons of construction seemed headed for obscurity and disuse, but the textualist revolution in statutory construction beginning late in the twentieth century that we discussed in the last chapter has changed that: the canons now play a significant role in debates over statutory meaning.

Legislative history provides a second resource for dealing with ambiguous texts. Statutes usually become laws only after a great deal of talk—committee hearings, reports, colloquies on the floor of the legislative body, perhaps most importantly changes in the statutory language under consideration as it progresses through the legislative process, or in contrast to earlier statutes. Somewhat similar processes surround the creation of other sorts of law such as administrative regulations. Although the traditional common law rule was that a court, at any rate, did not cite this sort of legislative history in interpreting a statute, that rule eventually disappeared in the United States. Indeed, by the 1970s American lawyers and judges made so much use of legislative history that British lawyers joked that an American court looked at the words of the statute only if its legislative history was unclear. The prominence of legislative history has waned due to the rise of textualism just as the canons of construction have waxed in significance. But despite the efforts of Justice Scalia and a few others to ban outright all references to legislative history, it remains part of the smart lawyer's statutory construction toolkit.

A third way of dealing with an unclear statutory text involves the invocation of the statute's (or the legislature's) purpose. For centuries, Anglo-American lawyers have talked cheerfully about following the mind or intention of the legislature or the purpose of the statute, without worrying too much about what "mind" or "intention" or "purpose" means in this context. In recent years, lawyers and judges have become much more self-conscious about what a court is doing and should be doing when the meaning of the statute is debatable. The more stringent versions of statutory textualism emphasize what we might call the written-ness of the statute: the only thing that the legislature made law was the words it enacted, and interpretation of those words must above all else respect the legislative decision to enact those words and no others. That view is sometimes buttressed by the assertion that it is a sheer fiction to refer to the purpose or intention of a multi-member (and sometimes multi-body) legislature.

On the other side of the spectrum are lawyers who adhere to what is sometimes called purposivism: their response to the strict textualists is that law doesn't exist for its own sake, and that a collective body such as a legislature may not have a single mind, but it can share a common purpose. The words of the statute must be read to achieve that purpose wherever that is possible. "The Legislature has the power to decide what the policy of the law shall be, and if it has intimated its will, however indirectly, that will should be recognized and obeyed."[13] The debate between strict(er) textualists and broad(er) purposivists is ongoing and, I suspect, irresolvable even in principle since the basic idea underlying each position—the words alone are the statute; a statute has a purpose and words can be an imperfect means of fully conveying that purpose—are true.

Let me conclude our discussion of statutory construction with an example. In 1993, the United States Supreme Court decided a case called *Smith v. United States*. *Smith* involved a federal statute requiring the imposition of specified penalties if the government proves that "during and in relation to any... drug trafficking crime," the defendant "use[d] or carrie[d] a firearm." Mr. Smith was convicted of drug trafficking crimes and the trial court imposed the additional penalty because Smith had "used" a gun in relation to a drug trafficking offense: specifically, he had tried to trade the gun for some cocaine. Smith's argument to the high Court was that what Congress meant to punish was the use of a gun *as a weapon*, not as the purchase price for illegal substances. A divided Supreme Court rejected Smith's argument and held that the statute cov-

---

13. *Johnson v. United States*, 163 Fed. 30, 32 (1st Cir. 1908) (Holmes, Circuit Justice).

ered his "gun for drugs" situation. The majority noted that "the words 'as a weapon' appear nowhere in the statute" and concluded that "use" therefore means "use," period.

> When a word is not defined by statute, we normally construe it in accord with its ordinary or natural meaning. Surely petitioner's treatment of his [gun] can be described as "use" within the everyday meaning of that term. Petitioner "used" his [gun] in an attempt to obtain drugs by offering to trade it for cocaine. Webster's defines "to use" as "[t]o convert to one's service" or "to employ." ... Petitioner's handling of the [gun] in this case falls squarely within those definitions.

The majority justices added that they did not think "Congress would have intended courts... to draw a fine metaphysical distinction between a gun's role in a drug offense as a weapon and its role as an item of barter."[14]

The dissenting justices, with the strong textualist Antonin Scalia writing, thought this reasoning remarkably obtuse:

> To use an instrumentality ordinarily means to use it for its intended purpose. When someone asks, "Do you use a cane?," he is not inquiring whether you have your grandfather's silver-handled walking stick on display in the hall; he wants to know whether you walk with a cane. Similarly, to speak of "using a firearm" is to speak of using it for its distinctive purpose, i.e., as a weapon. To be sure, "one can use a firearm in a number of ways," including as an article of exchange, just as one can "use" a cane as a hall decoration—but that is not the ordinary meaning of "using" the one or the other.[15]

Both the majority and the dissenters insisted that theirs was the proper reading of the statute's words; each paid careful attention to those words; each claimed fidelity to the statute's purpose. Both cannot have been right legally.[16]

---

14. *Smith v. United States*, 508 U.S. 223, 228–29, 240 (1993).

15. *Id.* at 242 (Scalia, J., dissenting).

16. There is, of course, no ambiguity about which reading of the statute is legally controlling after *Smith*. Even if you think the dissenters had the better of the argument, the majority's position prevailed. But that doesn't prevent you or me from concluding that

How to Do Things with Cases

At the heart of contemporary American lawtalk are the ways that American lawyers think and talk about cases. That is nothing new: as you know, the centrality of judicial decisions is an inheritance from English and earlier American legal history. To be sure, the ultimate controlling authority with respect to most present-day legal issues is a statute or regulation or constitutional provision or some other text that is law in itself. But as you also know, even in the many situations where that is true, the law in action, the law that a court or official is actually supposed to apply, is often to be found in, or worked out from, the precedents. If you want to know what sort of conduct is governed by the federal statute at issue in *Smith v. United States*, it won't do simply to read the words of the statute: what those words mean in action is what *Smith* (and other precedents construing the statute) have said that they mean.

In the older English common law, judicial decisions were usually said not to be the law themselves but only evidence of the law. This distinction made little sense after the development of a strong doctrine of *stare decisis* over the course of the nineteenth century: by 1909 the distinguished Harvard law professor John Chipman Gray could write that the "rules . . . laid down and applied by the courts" are "the Law."[17] This did not mean, and still doesn't, that a judicial opinion is law in the same way that a statute or regulation is law. As we've seen—but the point is so crucial that it bears repeating—the crucial difference is that the very words of the statute or regulation are the law, while the wording of a judicial decision, even the opinion of the Court for a unanimous Supreme Court, is not. The great English judge Lord Mansfield commented in 1762 that "[t]he reason and spirit of cases make law; not the letter of particular precedents."[18] In a very general sense (don't press this too far), when you try to figure out the law stated by a statute what you are doing is interpreting the meaning of the statute's language, but when you try to figure out the law stated by a judicial decision, you're working out how the line of reasoning the court applied to those facts, then, should be

---

the majority was wrong, and a state supreme court with an identically worded state statute would be free to follow Justice Scalia's reasoning.

17. John Chipman Gray, *The Nature and Sources of the Law* 102 (2d ed. 1921) (1st ed. 1909).

18. *Fisher v. Prince*, 97 Eng. Rep. 876, 876 (K.B. 1762).

applied to these facts, now. It is the idea of *stare decisis* that makes the decision law. So when we talk about how to use the law found in judicial decisions, we are talking about how to deal with precedent.[19]

I'm going to divide my comments on this into two sections: how do we analyze a precedent, and what can we do with it once we've analyzed it?

(1) How do we determine the law that was announced in a case that is, or may be, a controlling precedent? The traditional answer is to separate out what the opinion of the court says into holding and dicta (singular: dictum)—short for *obiter dictum*, "that which is said in passing." To make that distinction work, of course, we need to understand what the crucial terms mean. One way to define the *holding* of a decision is that it consists of whatever in the court's opinion is necessary to provide a legal justification or rationale for the judgment to which the court came: put another and even briefer way, the holding is whatever reasoning is necessary to support the result, the *ratio decidendi*, "the rationale for what was decided." Everything else is dicta. Simple, right? Unfortunately, not so much.

Think about *Smith v. United States*, the statutory case about using a firearm in connection with a drug trafficking offense. The bare decision there was that the statute applies when the gun in question was used as the purchase price for drugs, although not as a weapon. Sometimes people use the word "holding" for that sort of description of a case, but it's really just the result. What parts of the *Smith* majority's reasoning were necessary to support that result? The opinion of the Court tells the reader (1) that when a statute doesn't define a term, the term receives its "ordinary or natural meaning," (2) that the defendant's attempt to trade his gun for cocaine was "using a firearm" within the definitions of "to use" found in Webster's dictionary and elsewhere, (3) that the statute doesn't limit the potential scope of "to use" by including the words "as a weapon" or something to that effect, and (4) that giving "use" its broad meaning is more consistent with what the majority thinks Congress "would have intended." All four of these propositions support the Court's

19. Technically, the decision of a trial court is not a precedent, at least in the federal judicial system: "a district court decision does not have stare decisis effect; it is not a precedent.... It may be a wise, well-reasoned decision that persuades by the quality of its reasoning, but in that respect it is no different from a persuasive article or treatise." *Midlock v. Apple Vacations West, Inc.*, 406 F.3d 453, 457 (7th Cir. 2005).

decision, but couldn't you come to the same conclusion on the basis, say, just of the "natural meaning" and Webster's dictionary points? Or what about relying solely on the dictionary definition and congressional intent arguments? Which points are dicta and which part of the holding? Until some later decision clarifies the holding of *Smith*, there are several possible ways of stating the holding in *Smith*. Which is the most persuasive argument to make if you are a lawyer in a later case involving a similar issue may be a tricky question to answer, and the same is true if you are a judge whose only concern is to get the law right.

The existence of multiple answers to the problem of how to state the holding in *Smith* doesn't mean that all the possible answers, as to *Smith* or any other case, are equally plausible, but it does illustrate the fact that figuring out what is holding and what is dicta is not a mechanical process. Instead, even this most basic task in analyzing a case involves the exercise of judgment, judgment about what is the best way to understand the reasoning in the precedent, and judgment about what is most likely to persuade a future decisionmaker about the precedent's rightful application. The meaning of a precedent is not a fixed sum that you can calculate from its language.

Furthermore, the importance of a precedent for you and me as lawyers sometimes lies not in its holding at all, but in some other aspect of the case that may be dicta in a technical sense. In *United States v. Carolene Products Co.* (1938), for example, the US Supreme Court rejected a constitutional challenge to an act of Congress prohibiting the interstate shipment of "filled milk" against the claim that it violated the manufacturer's rights under the Fifth Amendment Due Process Clause.[20] For the Court, Justice Harlan Fiske Stone explained that "regulatory legislation affecting ordinary commercial transactions" is presumptively rational and unless that presumption is rebutted the courts will uphold the statute: *Carolene Products*'s Fifth Amendment *holding* is limited to that statement and application of due process rational basis scrutiny.

In a footnote, however, Stone addressed several hypothetical situations. Where a statute appears to violate an express constitutional prohi-

20. "Filled milk" is "skimmed milk compounded with any fat or oil other than milk fat, so as to resemble milk or cream." 304 U.S. 144, 146 (1938). The Court was equally unpersuaded by the argument that the statute was not a valid exercise of Congress's power to regulate interstate commerce.

bition, or "restricts those political processes which can ordinarily be expected to bring about repeal of undesirable legislation," or may stem from "prejudice against discrete and insular minorities," Stone suggested that "more searching judicial scrutiny" might be appropriate. Footnote four is the sheerest of dicta: it was entirely unnecessary to the decision, it addressed issues not before the Court, and it posed questions rather than declared answers. But it is footnote four that has played an important role in later debates.[21]

Mentioning *Carolene Products* brings up one last wrinkle to the task of analyzing precedents: is there anything at all you can do as a lawyer or judge with the opinions in a controlling precedent that aren't the opinion of the court?[22] Justice Stone's opinion in *Carolene Products* spoke for the Court... mostly... but the section with footnote four wasn't joined by a majority of the justices. Sometimes the majority of a court's judges can't agree at all on a single opinion. It is axiomatic in the American legal system that a decision must have a rationale and an appellate decision must be a meaningful holding that can serve as precedent. In the absence of an opinion of the court, the rationale and holding must be divined from the tea leaves provided by the various opinions that support the court's judgment. (Important note: there is no guarantee that the opinion announcing the court's judgment will provide the answer.) This confusing situation occurs with enough frequency on the United States Supreme Court that the Court has evolved a rule for dealing with it. "When a fragmented Court decides a case and no single rationale explaining the result enjoys the assent of five Justices, the holding of the Court may be viewed as that position taken by those Members who con-

---

21. 404 U.S. at 152 n.4. As if we didn't have enough formal reasons for dismissing footnote four, as noted in the text, the footnote wasn't even in the part of Justice Stone's opinion that was "of the Court"—one member of Stone's bare majority expressly noted that he didn't join that section of the opinion. The footnote hasn't got a shred of precedential force on its own; it's the ideas that have interested later constitutional lawyers, including some judges.

22. In addition to straightforward concurring and dissenting opinions, other, rarer species of appellate opinion can be found. The most common is perhaps the opinion "concurring in the judgment," a label indicating that the writer actually disagrees with at least part of the reasoning of the majority. Of course, if there is no majority opinion, all the opinions by judges in the majority are logically concurrences in the judgment, although the lead opinion announcing the court's decision is not labelled that way.

curred in the judgments on the narrowest grounds." This *Marks* rule isn't perfect, but other appellate courts follow a similar practice.[23]

Even when there *is* something labeled the opinion of the court, it doesn't follow that separate opinions are irrelevant to a lawyer stating the meaning of the case, or a judge seeking to apply the precedent to the case before her. One of the classic functions of a concurrence is to limit the scope of a precedent: the concurring judge may agree with what is said in the majority opinion but want to indicate that there are limits to how far the majority's reasoning should be taken. In *Smith v. United States*, for example, one of the majority justices filed a brief concurrence explaining that he thought the Court's decision was limited to construing the statutory word "uses" and that *Smith* was therefore not a precedent as to the meaning of other words in the statute.[24] Another familiar use of the concurrence is the opposite, to encourage future courts to develop further the line of reasoning that supports today's decision. In either situation, the concurrence implies that, respectively, a narrow or expansive understanding of the decision is consistent with respecting the decision as precedent. A lawyer interested in shaping how a precedent will be viewed by a later court (i.e., any good litigator) is often wise to pay close attention to a concurrence.

A dissenter by definition disagrees with the result in the case. Everything she writes is dicta. (This can get very complicated, especially on the US Supreme Court where the justices not infrequently file opinions with headings like "concurring in part, and in the judgment, and dissenting in part.") Dissents have many purposes. In statutory cases, the dissenter may be trying to alert the legislature to the mess the majority is making of the law. A dissent may be designed to blunt the enthusiasm of later courts for extending the reach of the decision, or to make it harder in other jurisdictions for the case to be treated as persuasive authority. And many dissents are appeals to the future, written in the hope that at some later time the dissenter's own court, or a higher court if there is one, will come to see that the dissenter had the better of the argument. This not infrequently happens, and sometimes what was originally a dissent becomes the law. Justice Holmes's opinion in the 1919 decision *Abrams v. United States* is the fountainhead of modern

23. *Marks v. United States*, 430 U.S. 188, 193 (1977).

24. *See Smith*, 508 U.S. at 241 (Blackmun, J., concurring).

free speech thinking; originally it was a dissent joined only by Justice Louis Brandeis. The same transmogrification of an originally separate opinion can occur with concurrences as well: the lead opinion on the relationship between the respective constitutional powers of Congress and the president is Justice Robert H. Jackson's opinion in *Youngstown Sheet & Tube Co. v. Sawyer* (1952), a concurrence joined at the time by no other justice.[25]

You may have noticed that I carefully named the three justices involved in the two opinions just discussed. That wasn't an historical flourish, or merely a reflection of the fact that legal citation form requires us to identify the author of a separate opinion. Holmes, Brandeis, and Jackson are big figures in the history of constitutional law and US Supreme Court decision making. The fact that it was a Holmes or Jackson who wrote, or a Brandeis who agreed, can add persuasive force to a position based on a separate opinion for an advocate who wants to rely on the opinion, or a judge seeking the best understanding of the law. In analyzing a precedent, it is obviously a mistake to confuse what is binding from what isn't, but it can also be a mistake to ignore powerful arguments that the case brings up merely because they aren't part of the holding.

(2) So, we've analyzed our precedent and know what we think is the right (or more persuasive) description of its meaning. Now where do we go with it? For the moment, let's assume we're representing a client in litigation. There are, basically, four ways we can argue about a case that seems relevant on its face: we can draw an analogy from the precedent to our situation, we can argue that the case establishes controlling doctrine, we can distinguish the precedent, or we can argue that it ought to be limited or overruled. Let's take each of those in turn.

If the precedent as we have analyzed it is favorable to our client, we're going to want to argue that it applies to our case, that the precedent is analogous to our case in so significant a fashion that it is relevant to or even determinative of the outcome—in other words, our client wins because this is *the* controlling precedent. There is more than one way in which a precedent can be analogous to a later case. Sometimes, the analogy resides squarely in the facts. Think, once again, of *Smith v. United*

25. *See Abrams v. United States*, 250 U.S. 616, 624–31 (1919) (Holmes, J., dissenting); *Youngstown Sheet & Tube Co. v. Sawyer*, 363 U.S. 579, 634–55 (1952) (Jackson, J., concurring).

States, and imagine yourself the Assistant US Attorney prosecuting a drug-trafficking case against Jones. In your case, Jones propped open a door with a gun while making a drug deal. In all likelihood, it is in the interests of your client (the United States) to put the defendant away for as long as the law allows, and the facts in *Smith* and *Jones* are very similar. *Smith* is analogous to your case, and you will argue to the trial court that Jones is subject to the "using a firearm" penalty. The two cases are analogous—though you are more likely to say that they are "indistinguishable" or even that "they are on all fours" with one another.[26]

Most analogies from precedent to current case aren't so simple, and involve the argument that some aspect of the reasoning in the precedent applies in the current case as well. *Smith* provides all sorts of possibilities in this regard: the Court's reasoning includes general propositions (statutory terms are given their "ordinary or natural meaning") and specific ones (the meaning of "to use" includes "to employ"). The opinion of the Court states or implies that certain kinds of argument are more or less persuasive: the majority cites Webster's for the meaning of "to use," which implies that it is appropriate to consult Webster's or some other widely used dictionary in establishing the definition of a statutory term.

The analogy may be more complex, and depend less on details. Recall that the *Smith* majority opinion tells us that the Court thought it unlikely Congress would have intended to make judges and juries draw "fine metaphysical distinctions" in deciding if a defendant had used a firearm. Zoom out from the specific issue in *Smith*, and the case might become support for the argument that courts should give a potentially ambiguous law whichever interpretation is simplest and most conducive to achieving the legislature's overall purpose. By means of conceptual analogy, a precedent can be extended to legal controversies and factual patterns far removed from its own specific issues.[27]

Some precedents lay down what the court clearly intends to be doctrine. By "doctrine" I mean a judicially constructed pattern of analysis that an appellate court intends to govern future cases raising the same general issue. The phenomenon occurs in all areas of caselaw. A good

---

26. My Jones hypothetical comes from Justice Scalia, although he used it for a different purpose. *See Smith*, 508 U.S. at 244 n.2 (Scalia, J., dissenting).

27. For more on analogical reasoning in the law, see Lloyd Weinreb's great book *Legal Reason: The Use of Analogy in Legal Argument* (2d ed. 2016).

example is *Van Dyke v. Glover*, a case where the Arkansas Supreme Court faced the old issue of when the courts should give a remedy for a broken promise in a situation that didn't fit the paradigm of a formal commercial bargain. For reasons we don't need to discuss, the plaintiffs couldn't prove that they had an enforceable deal—in that respect they were like the sister in *Kirksey v. Kirksey*, and they were like her as well in that they alleged facts showing they had relied to their detriment on the defendants' promise. But the date was 1996, not 1845, and unlike Justice Ormond's colleagues in *Kirksey*, the Arkansas court had accepted detrimental reliance as a valid basis for enforcing a promise in earlier decisions. What *Van Dyke* added was a more precise statement of when reliance will suffice: the court characterized as the relevant "blackletter rule" the principle stated in section 90 of the Restatement, Second of Contracts:

> A promise which the promisor should reasonably expect to induce action or forbearance on the part of the promisee or a third person and which does induce such action or forbearance is binding if injustice can be avoided only by enforcement of the promise.[28]

By formally approving section 90's formulation of the principle, *Van Dyke v. Glover* created what I mean by doctrine: the pattern of thought and argument a court should follow to determine liability in such situations. Is there a promise? Reasonable expectation that it will induce action or forbearance? Success in the inducement? Injustice if the promise is not enforced? When *Van Dyke* is relevant at all, its force as precedent is likely to be the way that it lays out this line of reasoning. Whether you and I think the doctrine helps or hurts our client's case, we are stuck with using it... unless, of course, we can distinguish *Van Dyke*.

Which brings us to distinguishing cases, the third thing that one can do with a precedent. Distinguishing a case is the opposite of analogizing from it: we distinguish a decision by arguing that because of some factual or conceptual dissimilarity with the case we are considering, there is no sound analogy. What appears to be a controlling precedent therefore doesn't control at all. After *Smith v. United States*, a defendant clearly can't the avoid the "using a firearm" statute simply by pointing out that

28. *Van Dyke v. Glover*, 326 Ark. 736, 744–45 (1996).

he didn't use the gun as a weapon...but what if the firearm in question is an eighteenth-century musket missing its barrel? You could still hit someone over the head with it, but is a gun a "firearm" when it self-evidently cannot be fired? I don't know what the Supreme Court would say, but if I were defense counsel I would argue vigorously that *Smith* is distinguishable. After all, Smith could have fired his gun if the situation went wrong from his perspective, while my client's musket is just a long stick of wood.

Fourth, we come to what is usually the most desperate expedient in dealing with a case, the direct argument that it should not be given precedential force but, instead, limited to its facts or overruled. The first thing to remember is that an inferior court can't overrule precedents from a court higher up in the relevant judicial hierarchy. If there is a plausible argument for doing so, the lower court can distinguish the higher court's decision, but if that's not possible, the lower court must follow the precedent. Even when you're arguing to the court that made the precedent, furthermore, persuading it that it made a mistake and should repudiate its earlier decision is usually a heavy lift: better by far, most of the time, to distinguish the earlier case and thereby invite the court both to pay homage to its own earlier wisdom and rule for your client.

There are many other things to be said about how lawyers do things with cases. Stay tuned for the rest of law school, and beyond.[29]

Talking about the Relationship between Institutions

In chapter two, I pointed out that the old English common law was obsessively concerned with procedure, so much so that arguments over whether the plaintiff should have proceeded in trespass or in covenant tended to drown out overt discussion about whether and when the legal system ought to give such a plaintiff a remedy. One of the great transformations in law that took place over the course of the nineteenth century, as we saw in chapter three, was the rise of a substantive law of torts, contracts, and so on. But this change didn't mean that the old concern with procedure disappeared, and in particular interest in those

29. For more about *stare decisis*, see the endnote.

procedural concepts and rules that govern the relationship between legal institutions. In concluding this chapter, I want to mention three important concepts in contemporary lawtalk that concern issues of institutional relationship.

Let's start with the distinction between law and fact. A non-lawyer would be tempted, I suspect, to think that in this distinction the world beyond the law forces itself onto the attention of the lawyers. Well, yes and no. Was the defendant negligent in driving into the ditch and knocking over the plaintiff's mailbox in the process? The answer to that question certainly involves which events occurred in the physical universe—the answer is no if the defendant and his car were a hundred miles away at the time, although even such a fact needs to be established through the forms and procedures of the law. But the question of the defendant's negligence is not just a matter of proving physical events: negligence is a legal concept, typically defined as a failure to exercise the level of care that a reasonably prudent person would have used in similar circumstances. This legal concept of negligence maps onto the world of physical events, but in doing so it need not, and sometimes does not, follow what most non-lawyers would call carelessness. So, is the question "was the defendant negligent?" a question of fact or a question of law? The answer depends on how you want to allocate responsibilities among different legal institutions.

A question of fact goes to the jury or to the trial judge where there is a bench trial (i.e., where there is no jury). The decisions of the "trier of fact" are almost always very difficult for a reviewing court to disturb: the usual standard is some version of the "clear error rule:" the later, reviewing court can reject the trier of fact's conclusions only if they are blatantly wrong. In contrast, deciding a question of law is the task for the trial judge when there is a jury, and on appeal the reviewing court is free to reverse simply because the appellate judges think the trial judge was wrong. Now consider the choices: if we call negligence a question of fact, in the vast majority of cases whatever the trier of fact decides about the defendant's negligence will be the legal system's final answer, while if we label negligence a question of law, the reviewing judges will have much broader latitude to substitute their views for the original conclusion. Different American jurisdictions have come to different conclusions on which is the better institutional arrangement, and there are ways to split the difference by treating negligence as a mixed question of law and fact.

Let's be clear: whichever choice we make, nothing about negligence itself necessarily changes—in any event it will always involve both physical facts and a legal standard. Whether we call it law or fact or confusingly both has to do with institutions and their relationship.

This business of reviewability, moreover, is not limited to the fact/law distinction: across the board, the law structures the extent to which a reviewing court may substitute its views for those expressed in the judgment it is reviewing. Here's an example, from a federal appeals court decision chosen almost at random. The court of appeals began its analysis by stating that "we review the district court's factual findings for clear error, its legal conclusions de novo, and its exercise of equitable judgment for abuse of discretion."[30] Never mind for now what any of that means: I just want you to note the appearance (once again) of the fact/law distinction, and of three distinct standards of review, each of which structures the relationship between the trial and appellate courts in a different way.

Even the idea of a burden of proof is, in part, a tool for deciding which institution within the legal system is responsible for some aspect of the ultimate decision. Take the familiar language about proof "beyond a reasonable doubt" that states the government's burden of proof when it prosecutes someone for a crime. The beyond a reasonable doubt standard is often praised as a protection for liberty, and so it is, but it protects liberty by imposing duties on different legal actors: on the prosecutor who has the ethical duty of determining whether she thinks she can meet the burden, on the jury that has the legal duty to decide if she has done so, on up to the appellate court which, in the federal system, must decide not if the judges think the defendant guilty beyond a reasonable doubt, but instead whether a reasonable jury could have thought so. Here, as elsewhere in twenty-first century American law, much of what we lawyers talk about concerns not the substance of the law, but the question of who gets to decide an issue. Lord Coke would not have been surprised.

★ ★ ★

Someone once wrote that "No one can become a good lawyer—let alone a great one—who is not willing to subject himself to the unpleas-

30. *DISH Network Serv. L.L.C. v. Laducer*, 725 F.3d 877, 881 (8th Cir. 2013).

ant discipline of achieving a high degree of professional competence.... We must pay great attention to nuts and bolts and other uninteresting things."[31] I think he was overstating the negatives, but there is no getting around the fact that a modern American legal education has its occasional moments of tedium—occasional, mind you!! Tedious or not, the nuts and bolts that I have been talking about in this chapter are essential elements in a legal education. They are the tools the profession and the legal system provide lawyers so that the lawyers in turn may play a socially important role in the human world beyond the law. A great legal education is not one that invites the student to ignore that broader world in the pursuit of merely technical competence, but setting the student on the path to technical competence is crucial. The great legal scholar Karl Llewellyn liked to say that "Technique without ideals is a menace, but ideals without technique are a mess." I think Prof. Llewellyn was right: in the law, technique and ideals are inseparable.[32]

---

31. Grant Gilmore, What is a Law School?, 15 Conn. L. Rev. 1, 3 (1982).

32. Karl N. Llewellyn, On What is Wrong with So-Called Legal Education, 35 Colum. L. Rev. 651, 662 (1935).

Conclusion: The Law as a Calling

Holmes, one last time. Learned Hand, a distinguished federal judge and a friend of Holmes, once teasingly exhorted Holmes, who was on his way to the Supreme Court justices' weekly meeting to discuss cases, "Do justice!" Holmes responded: "That is not my job. My job is to play the game according to the rules."[1]

Some readers of this book may feel that Holmes's response illustrates a deep problem with American law.[2] We have discussed many aspects of the American legal tradition, but we have spent little time addressing questions of justice, or the other great moral themes that most of us would see, or hope to see, in the law—liberty, equality, the common good, and general welfare. The two most significant moral issues that the book addresses at any length are the law's failure to address slavery before the Civil War, and its role in dismantling Reconstruction afterwards. If that is all one can say, a reasonable conclusion might be that the law is not a profession fit for a morally serious person. But that is *not* all that can be said about the relationship between law and justice, and it is not the conclusion I propose to leave you with.

Look again at Holmes's response to Hand. Holmes doesn't actually say that the law is unrelated to morality or deny that the goal of the legal system is justice. His words address his role in the system, his "job." Furthermore, "job" was a loaded term for Holmes. It connoted modest,

1. Learned Hand, *The Spirit of Liberty* 306–07 (Irving Dilliard ed., 3d ed. 1960).

2. Others, to be sure, may think the problem lies with the book!

practical, and nontransformative goals along with an intense concern for craft and professionalism. Holmes liked to talk about his imaginary "'Society of Jobbists,' whose members [acted with] concentrated and craftsmanlike attention to the task at hand. Jobbists believed that in doing 'one's job as well as one can, one achieves practical altruism.'"[3] "Playing the game according to the rules," making legal decisions based on the judge's conscientious application of the recognized and shared tools of legal thought to the case before the court, is precisely what judges are supposed to be doing.

American law does not recognize the legitimacy of decisions that are arrived at in any other way. "A ... distinctive feature of adjudication is that the court's decision is to be based entirely on the law.... What are appropriate sources of the law is a question about which there is much disagreement, but no one doubts that a court is to look to those sources and nowhere else."[4] In litigating a case or advising a client, furthermore, other lawyers rely on the judges' observance of this principle. Put another way, the judges' commitment to playing the game according to the rules makes it possible for other lawyers to do all the other jobs that American society permits or assigns to members of the profession, including the job—for some lawyers—of advocating transformative change in the law. The ability of the American legal system to achieve justice or any other moral goal thus rests on American lawyers' adherence, in each of their roles, to norms of craftsmanship and good faith. In this way, the individual lawyer's attention to sound legal reasoning and professional conduct serves the cause of justice in the United States whatever that lawyer's particular job or other moral commitments.

A critical reader might respond that this answer, however true, somewhat misses the point. Yes, the critic concedes, I see that there is a kind of internal role-morality that judges and other lawyers need to observe, and I'll even grant that their doing so plays an indirect role in achieving justice by keeping the legal system in good working order. But for all you've said, a well-functioning legal system might just as easily serve as a tool for achieving injustice—you said as much in chapter three's discussion of slavery. Is or is not American law committed to substantive justice, true liberty, genuine equality? Or is it morally neutral on those great questions?

3. Michael Herz, *"Do Justice!": Variations of A Thrice-Told Tale*, 82 Va. L. Rev. 111, 130 (1996).

4. Weinreb, *Legal Reason: The Use of Analogy in Legal Argument* 50–51 (2d ed. 2016).

My answer has three parts. First, it is possible to overstate the distinction between the law's internal morality and substantive or extra-legal norms of justice. A court that adheres in good faith to the principle of *stare decisis* will in doing so avoid the risk of treating similarly situated parties differently because of the judges' perhaps subconscious biases. Playing the game according to the rules often makes it difficult or impossible to perpetrate substantive injustice.[5]

Second, American law incorporates or embodies many substantive moral norms because they are norms that are widely accepted across the American political community. Detailing these many points of moral and legal agreement would make this a *much* longer book and transform it into a treatise on the substance of American law in general.

Finally, to the extent readers still think that I have portrayed a legal system that creates substantial room for moral disagreement, they are right. It is a central feature of the American system of law that on many issues the system can serve divergent and indeed contradictory moral viewpoints, depending on which viewpoint is held by people with the legitimate institutional authority to act.[6] But this is a virtue, not a bug in the system. The legal system of the United States "is made for people of fundamentally differing views," and it provides the institutional means by which Americans can remain a political *community* even though there are issues on which some Americans hold "opinions that [other Americans] loathe and believe to be fraught with death."[7] American law leaves open ample room for moral disagreement not because it is essentially amoral but out of two profound moral commitments, to truth as the only satisfactory basis for political and legal decision making, and to "freedom of thought and speech" as "the matrix, the indispensable condition, of nearly every other form of freedom."[8] An essential element of justice is the recognition that much of the time others may reasonably disagree.

---

5. Yes, I am presupposing a contestable view of what justice entails. There is no escape from normative thinking in the law.

6. The possibility that one or the other side in a moral dispute might achieve legal victory by corrupting the law's institutions is real but beside the point. Corruption and abuse of power are ever-present possibilities in any human political or legal system.

7. The quoted words are from *Lochner v. New York*, 198 U.S. 45, 76 (1905) (Holmes, J., dissenting) and *Abrams v. United States*, 250 U.S. 616, 630 (1919) (Holmes, J., dissenting). Hmm... I guess Judge Hand's anecdote wasn't quite Holmes's last appearance.

8. *Palko v. State of Connecticut*, 302 U.S. 319, 326–27 (1937) (Cardozo, J., for the Court). The first part of the sentence paraphrases Holmes's discussion of "the theory of our Constitution" in his *Abrams* dissent, 250 U.S. at 630.

One need only remember that there was once an American law of slavery to dismiss any suggestion that the American legal tradition is a story of the flawless accomplishment of perfect justice. And you like I no doubt have a list of current evils that American law tolerates or even exacerbates—although our lists may not be identical! The American legal system and American lawyers, past and present, are flawed and fallible, and if you become a member of the bar, you will take on the personal, ethical responsibility to "seek improvement of the law, access to the legal system, the administration of justice, and the quality of service rendered by the legal profession."[9] A lively awareness of what is wrong with the law is part of an American lawyer's calling, and the shared commitment to address those problems is part of what makes the profession an honorable one. When the United States Supreme Court recognized, in *Brown v. Board of Education* (1954), that *de jure* racial segregation is an egregious violation of the Constitution, it vindicated not only the moral idealism of the lawyers who persuaded it, but their professionalism and lawyerly skills as well.[10]

Much that you study in the first year in law school can seem quite remote from high questions of justice and law reform, and even from the more particular concerns at stake in the business transactions or intellectual property litigation or estate planning or regulatory agency work that you hope to do after graduation. But do not be fooled: the 1L year is the critically important period in which people are immersed in the legal tradition and thereby begin, proverbially, to think like lawyers and thus able to pursue not only professional success but equal justice under law. What students learn in those first two semesters provides the foundations for everything else in law school and beyond. The purpose of this book is to aid the reader in laying those foundations.

9. N.C. Rules of Prof'l Conduct preamble 0.1(6). I quote my own bar's language, but all state bars impose similar ethical responsibilities.

10. For a succinct description of the ways in which the great civil rights lawyers Charles Hamilton Houston and Thurgood Marshall and their colleagues combined ideals, craftsmanship and courage in their long legal campaign to bring the Court to *Brown*, *see* H. Jefferson Powell, The Road from *Plessy* to *Brown*, in Powell, *The Practice of American Constitutional Law* 199–202 (2022). (Marshall was, of course, later a Supreme Court justice.)

Endnotes

Oliver Wendell Holmes (1841–1935). The son of a famous Boston physician and man of letters, Dr. Oliver Wendell Holmes, Sr.,[1] Holmes graduated from Harvard College just in time to volunteer to serve in the Union Army, where he was severely wounded three times and almost died of dysentery. He subsequently studied law at Harvard and in a cousin's law office and practiced law for about fifteen years. While in practice, Holmes also carried out an intensive program of legal and legal history scholarship that culminated in his 1880 lectures on the common law. The trans-Atlantic success of the lectures-turned-book led to an endowed chair at the Harvard Law School, which Holmes accepted only to leave within a few months for a seat on the Massachusetts Supreme Judicial Court (1882–1902; chief justice from 1899). After his appointment to the United States Supreme Court, where he served from 1902 to 1932, Holmes's national reputation steadily rose, in large part because of his eloquent dissents. (He was sometimes called the Great Dissenter although, in fact, by twenty-first century standards he was slow to dissent.) Among his most important opinions are his dissents in *Lochner v. New York*, which derided the majority's decision striking down a maximum-hours law as "decided upon an economic theory which a large part of the country does not entertain," and in *Abrams v. United States*, which explained the First Amendment's protection of free speech through the metaphor of the marketplace of ideas: the amendment embodies the

1. Justice Holmes dropped his previous use of "Jr." in his name when his father died in 1894.

Constitution's "theory" that "the ultimate good desired is better reached by free trade in ideas—that the best test of truth is the power of the thought to get itself accepted in the competition of the market."[2]

At and immediately after his retirement Holmes enjoyed popular recognition and affection equaled by few if any other American judges. Since his death, Holmes has tended to be a controversial figure: the two radically different views of him quoted in footnote 2 in chapter one should give you a feeling for the range of opinions. The quotations are, respectively, from Professor Gilmore's *The Ages of American Law* and Judge Posner's introduction to *The Essential Holmes*. Even harsh critics, however, have to concede that Holmes is a major figure. For example, in an endnote in the book containing his savage description of Holmes, Professor Gilmore remarks that "Holmes, to the extent I can follow the dark outlines of his thought, seems to me to have been both a greater man and a more profound thinker than the mythical Holmes ever was."[3]

The Traditional Common Law Courts at Westminster. The history of the emergence in the Middle Ages of three central royal courts that sat to adjudicate various issues in the common law is complicated and not entirely clear. For the purposes of this book we need not delve into the details. The original distinction between the roles of the Court of King's (or Queen's) Bench and the Court of Common Pleas was that the latter originally heard cases in which the Crown had no proprietary interest; the barons of the somewhat later Court of Exchequer were particularly concerned with cases involving royal revenues. King's Bench and Common Pleas sat in Westminster Hall, while Exchequer was housed in an adjoining building. Each court generally sought to expand its jurisdiction, and the result was that their domains tended to overlap and shift over time. Life is complicated, however, and expanding a court's jurisdiction was not invariably a positive development from the perspective of that court's judges. In presenting a 1575 defamation action in the Court of Common Pleas, the reporter appended a note to an observation by Chief Justice James Dyer that if followed would have the effect of narrowing the scope of defamation liability in Common Pleas: Dyer

2. *Lochner v. New York*, 198 U.S. 45, 75 (1905) (Holmes, J., dissenting); *Abrams v. United States*, 250 U.S. 616, 630 (1919) (Holmes, J., dissenting).

3. Gilmore & Bobbitt, *Ages* 167. The quotations in the chapter one footnote are to *id.* at 44, and *The Essential Holmes* xxix–xxx (reordered).

"then said he wished such actions would go to the further end of the Hall (meaning the Queen's Bench)."[4]

The Court of Exchequer Chamber was an originally ad hoc, fifteenth-century arrangement given statutory form in 1585, which allowed for appeals from one of the three common law courts. Because the court was not a continuing body, its members were selected from among the judges of the Westminster courts.

Sir Edward Coke (1552–1634). Coke was a student in Trinity College, Cambridge but left without a degree to study law. He was called to the bar in 1578 after only six years in the Inner Temple (one of the four "Inns of Court" that were the focus of legal education in this period; it usually took eight years) and began a quick ascent to prominence as a barrister, in part because of his great learning. Coke entered government under Queen Elizabeth I as solicitor general (1592–94), speaker of the House of Commons (1593–94), and then attorney general (1594–1606) under Elizabeth and her successor King James I. As the main text indicates, Coke's tenure as chief justice of Common Pleas (1606–13) and King's Bench (1613–16) was stormy, and ended with his abrupt dismissal when he refused to bow to the king's wishes in a controversy over church matters.

After the king fired him, Coke quickly entered Parliament, where he was a thorn in the side both of James and of his successor Charles I. Coke's posthumous reputation as a great defender of liberty against Stuart tyranny was enhanced by his central role in drafting the 1628 Petition of Right, which both houses of Parliament approved and submitted to King Charles. The petition detailed the statutes Parliament claimed the Crown had violated and was a widely popular assertion of the "rights and liberties" of Englishmen. While the petition was being considered, Charles ordered the Commons not debate matters of state, an order that Coke disobeyed and denounced as contrary to parliamentary privilege.

During and after his service in government and on the bench, Coke found time to become a prolific scholar, compiling thirteen volumes of reports and writing a four-volume treatise titled *The Institutes of the Lawes of England*, the first volume of which appeared in 1628 and was a standard introductory text for would-be lawyers on both sides of the

4. *Anon.* (C.P. 1575), in Baker & Milsom, *Sources of English Legal History* 638.

Atlantic before (and then, at first, alongside) Blackstone's *Commentaries*. Coke's critics, from King James to the present, have sometimes accused him of using his (deserved) reputation for legal learning and his role as a reporter to skew the law in directions he favored, but whatever truth there is in the accusation has not historically damaged his image in American legal memory as "th[e] great defender of individual freedom and ancient rights."[5]

John Marshall (1755–1835). The son of a Virginia farmer and surveyor, Marshall joined the Continental Army early in the Revolutionary War and fought in several battles. While on leave, in 1780 Marshall attended Chancellor George Wythe's law lectures at the College of William & Mary and was admitted to the Virginia bar. After the War, Marshall pursued a successful two-track career in the law and Virginia politics, and in 1788 he was a delegate to the state convention that ratified the US Constitution. He declined appointment by President George Washington to be the first US attorney for Virginia and later to be attorney general, but in 1797 he accepted President John Adams's request to serve as one of three US commissioners to France. The mission proved a failure, which led in short order to an undeclared naval war with France, but Marshall received national acclaim when it became public knowledge that he and his colleagues had rebuffed French bullying and demands for bribes and a loan as a condition for serious negotiations (the so-called XYZ affair). Marshall subsequently served as Adam's secretary of state (1800–01) before Adams appointed him to be chief justice of the US Supreme Court, an office he held until his death.[6]

As the main text indicates, Marshall is a major figure in American legal history, and most particularly in the development of federal constitutional law and the institutional history of the US Supreme Court. The Court seemed almost insignificant for most of its first decade: the first chief justice, John Jay, resigned to become governor of New York and

---

5. *State ex rel. Knight v. Pub. Serv. Comm'n*, 161 W. Va. 447, 458 (1978).

6. Marshall was actually secretary and chief justice simultaneously for a month, a curious arrangement (to say the least) from a modern perspective and perhaps from his. By the way, Marshall's office in his lifetime was titled "Chief Justice of the Supreme Court of the United States." The first federal chief justice to use what is now the official title, "Chief Justice of the United States," was Salmon P. Chase in 1866. Chase gave himself the grander label on his own, but Congress acquiesced a few years later.

declined reappointment in 1800, explaining to President Adams that the federal judicial system was fatally defective.[7] During Marshall's first years on the bench, furthermore, the Court was the object of deep animosity on the part of President Thomas Jefferson (Marshall's cousin, ironically), but after James Madison succeeded Jefferson, the Court under Marshall's steady leadership emerged as an increasingly important actor in American government.

Chief Justice Marshall's opinion for a unanimous Court in *McCulloch v. Maryland* (1819) is arguably the most important constitutional law opinion ever written. In the early Republic, some prominent figures, one of them Jefferson, argued that the US Constitution should be construed in narrow, literalistic terms. In *McCulloch*, Marshall sweepingly rejected that view and created a very different framework for decision: the Constitution's "nature... requires, that only its great outlines should be marked, its important objects designated, and the minor ingredients which compose those objects, be deduced from the nature of the objects themselves... we must never forget that it is a *constitution* we are expounding." Another great judge, John Marshall Harlan II, later summarized Marshall's understanding of the Constitution as requiring a court to approach its text "not in a literalistic way, as if we had a tax statute before us, but as the basic charter of our society, setting out in spare but meaningful terms the principles of government."[8] Perhaps the best brief statement of Marshall's importance is then-Judge Cardozo's observation in his Yale lectures that "Marshall... gave to the constitution of the United States the impress of his own mind; and the form of our constitutional law is what it is, because he moulded it while it was still plastic and malleable in the fire of his own intense convictions."[9]

---

7. "I left the Bench perfectly convinced that under a System so defective," the federal judiciary "would not obtain the Energy weight and Dignity which are essential to its affording due support to the national Governmt.; nor acquire the public Confidence and Respect, which, as the last Resort of the Justice of the Nation, it should possess." Nothing, Jay continued, had changed. Jay, Letter to John Adams (Jan. 2, 1801), https://founders.archives.gov/documents/Adams/99-02-02-4745.

8. *McCulloch v. Maryland*, 17 U.S. (4 Wheat.) 316, 407 (1819); *Poe v. Ullman*, 367 U.S. 497, 540 (1961) (Harlan, J., concurring). This Justice Harlan, by the way, was the grandson of the justice who dissented from the decision upholding *de jure* racial segregation, *Plessy v. Ferguson*.

9. Cardozo, *The Nature of the Judicial Process* 169–70.

Benjamin N. Cardozo (1870–1938). Cardozo's father was a state judge in New York City who resigned in disgrace over a corruption scandal when Cardozo was two. Cardozo entered Columbia College when he was sixteen, and afterwards attended Columbia Law School although he left after two years without the degree, and had to wait briefly to be admitted to the bar since he wasn't quite old enough. He quickly became a highly successful litigator and advisor, and after twenty-three years in practice was still relatively young when he was elected to the New York Supreme Court (the state's trial court of general jurisdiction) and then transferred after a month to the Court of Appeals, the state's highest court. Cardozo served on that court from 1914 to 1932, from 1927 on as chief judge. In Cardozo's era, the New York Court of Appeals was unquestionably the greatest common law court in the United States. Among many famous opinions Cardozo wrote for the Court were *McPherson v. Buick Motor Co.* and *Palsgraf v. Long Island R. Co.*, milestones in modern tort law, and *Allegheny College v. Nat'l Chautauqua County Bank of Jamestown*, an important decision in the law of charitable subscriptions.[10] When Justice Holmes retired in January 1932, President Herbert Hoover (a Republican) nominated Cardozo to replace Holmes mostly because there was virtually universal agreement that only Cardozo could worthily do so. Cardozo's premature death in 1938 from a stroke following a heart attack limited his influence on federal law, but several of his constitutional law opinions brought the idea that legal questions are matters of degree to bear on hotly debated issues in a fashion that the Court quickly accepted.[11]

---

10. *McPherson*, 17 N.Y. 382 (1916), eliminated the "privity of contract" doctrine that protected a negligent product manufacturer from liability because the injured consumer did not buy the product directly from the manufacturer. *Palsgraf*, 248 N.Y. 339 (1928), denied a recovery in tort because the injury to the plaintiff was not reasonably foreseeable by the defendant. *Allegheny College*, 246 N.Y. 369 (1927), held that a promise to leave by will a gift to the plaintiff college that the promisor wished to be used to set up a scholarship fund in her name was enforceable because implicit in the promise and the parties' actions was a promise in return by the college to carry out the promisor's wishes.

11. *Compare A.L.A. Schechter Poultry Corp. v. United States*, 295 U.S. 495, 554 (1935) (Cardozo, J., concurring, joined by one other justice) ("The law is not indifferent to considerations of degree.") *with NLRB v. Jones & Laughlin Steel Corp.*, 301 U.S. 1, 37 (1937) (opinion of the Court joined by five justices) ("The question is necessarily one of degree.").

More on *Stare Decisis*. The doctrine of precedent or *stare decisis* ("stand by what is decided") is a basic building block of common law reasoning and decision making. "That doctrine imparts authority to a decision, depending on the court that rendered it, merely by virtue of the authority of the rendering court and independently of the quality of its reasoning. The essence of *stare decisis* is that the mere existence of certain decisions becomes a reason for adhering to their holdings in subsequent cases. The bare fact that a case has been decided is a ground for deciding the next case, if materially identical, in the same way."[12]

The federal judicial system follows precedent fairly straightforwardly. "Vertical" precedents (decisions by higher courts) always bind lower courts, so that decisions of the Supreme Court are binding on all other federal courts, and on all state courts as to questions of federal law, and the decisions of the relevant court of appeals bind a federal district court. The Supreme Court claims to apply "horizontal" *stare decisis* effect to its own decisions subject to its authority to make a principled decision to overrule a relevant precedent, and federal appeals courts do as well, but with a wrinkle: the federal circuits ordinarily decide cases in panels of three judges rather than *en banc*, and a later panel has no authority to overrule precedent set by an earlier panel or by the appeals court sitting *en banc*. Only the *en banc* court can do so. Finally, "a district court decision does not have stare decisis effect; it is not a precedent. It may be a wise, well-reasoned decision that persuades by the quality of its reasoning, but in that respect it is no different from a persuasive article or treatise. The fact of such a decision is not a reason for following it."[13] (Other doctrines such as estoppel and "the law of the case" sometimes forbid a party from challenging a trial court decision in the same or a related case.)

In addition, the federal courts treat precedent differently if the question at issue is a matter of statutory construction or constitutional law: "considerations of *stare decisis* have added force in statutory cases because Congress may alter what we have done by amending the statute. In constitutional cases, by contrast, Congress lacks this option, and an incorrect or outdated precedent may be overturned only by our own

12. *Midlock v. Apple Vacations West, Inc.*, 406 F.3d 453, 457 (7th Cir. 2005).

13. *Id.* at 457–58.

reconsideration or by constitutional amendment." For that reason, "adherence to precedent is not rigidly required in constitutional cases."[14]

State court systems generally follow similar rules.

But what if the relevant "horizontal" precedent was wrongly decided? "Respecting *stare decisis* means sticking to some wrong decisions.... Indeed, *stare decisis* has consequence only to the extent it sustains incorrect decisions; correct judgments have no need for that principle to prop them up. Accordingly, an argument that we got something wrong—even a good argument to that effect—cannot by itself justify scrapping settled precedent. Or otherwise said, it is not alone sufficient that we would decide a case differently now than we did then. To reverse course, we require as well what we have termed a 'special justification'—over and above the belief that the precedent was wrongly decided."[15]

The passage I just quoted states a commonplace in American law, but although it is the standard American view, it is not self-evidently correct. *Why* should a court persist in following what it now recognizes as error when it is not obliged to do so because the precedent comes from a superior court? The US Supreme Court's answer to this question is usually that "*stare decisis* is a principle of policy and not a mechanical formula of adherence to the latest decision"—there are both prudential and equitable grounds for treating like cases the same. (You will recall the lawyer's argument, ultimately unsuccessful to be sure, to the Court of Common Pleas in *Flaundres v. Rycheman*, which we discussed in chapter two: "I think you will do as others have done in the same case, or else we do not know what the law is.") A quite different answer would be that adherence to precedent is implicit in the basic understanding of adjudication that the American legal system took over from the English common law. "On the eighteenth-century view (most influentially expounded by Blackstone), the judge's duty to follow precedent derives from the nature of the judicial power itself.... [When a court] says to the bar, 'We may have decided this question the opposite way yesterday, but this does not

---

14. *Patterson v. McLean Credit Union*, 491 U.S. 164, 175 n. 1 (1989); *Arizona v. Rumsey*, 467 U.S. 203, 212 (1984).

15. *Kimble v. Marvel Ent., LLC*, 576 U.S. 446, 455–56 (2015).

bind us today,' such a statement exceeds the judicial power, which is based on reason, not *fiat*."[16]

One final wrinkle. In recent years US Supreme Court Justice Clarence Thomas has articulated an approach to both constitutional and statutory construction cases that goes a long way toward eliminating horizontal *stare decisis*, at least in the federal system and on the Supreme Court.

> Given that the primary role of federal courts today is to interpret legal texts with ascertainable meanings, precedent plays a different role in our exercise of the 'judicial Power' than it did at common law. In my view, if the Court encounters a decision that is demonstrably erroneous—*i.e.*, one that is not a permissible interpretation of the text—the Court should correct the error, regardless of whether other factors support overruling the precedent.... Although this case involves a constitutional provision, I would apply the same *stare decisis* principles to matters of statutory interpretation.[17]

Justice Thomas's basic rationale for this proposed change in the federal law of precedent is reminiscent of Robert Rantoul's attack on the common law: "A demonstrably incorrect judicial decision... is tantamount to *making* law, and adhering to it... perpetuates a usurpation of the legislative power."[18]

Read in the abstract, the change required by this approach to *stare decisis* might appear rather limited in scope. After all, it allows for adherence to a precedent that is "incorrect" but not "demonstrably" so because such a precedent (although mistaken) rests on "a textually permissible interpretation of the law." The problem with this limitation on the proposal is that its limiting force depends to a very great extent on the ad-

---

16. The judicial quotations are from, respectively, *Citizens United v. Fed. Election Comm'n*, 558 U.S. 310, 363 (2010) and *Anastasoff v. United States*, 23 F.3d 898, 901, 904–05 (8th Cir.) (cleaned up), *vacated as moot*, 235 F.3d 1054 (8th Cir. 2000). The *Anastasoff* opinion was written by a great judge, Richard S. Arnold, and his view that *stare decisis* is implicit in the (correct) understanding of the American idea of judicial power for historical reasons should not be dismissed out of hand, although it is not the mainstream view.

17. *Gamble v. United States*, 139 S.Ct. 1960, 1984, 1987 (2019) (Thomas, J., concurring). Justice Thomas expressly noted that he was not addressing the authority of vertical precedent in cases involving federal law questions. *See id.* at 1981 n. 2.

18. *Id.* at 1984 (Thomas, J., concurring). The quotations in the following paragraph are from the same page.

verb "demonstrably," which seems to have less to do with the intellectual force of the arguments for and against a precedent than with the certainty the critic feels about his position. How does a judge, trying in good faith to apply Justice Thomas's view, determine when her belief that the challenged precedent seems to have gotten the meaning of the constitutional or statutory provision wrong reaches the level that she can fairly say the precedent is *demonstrably* erroneous, particularly if other judges think the precedent within the range of "textually permissible interpretations?" There are, no doubt, constitutional and statutory decisions that most lawyers would agree are textually indefensible, but one suspects that most Supreme Court precedents will produce both intellectually serious defenders and critics. And this is to leave to one side the question whether all legitimate forms of legal argument, particularly in constitutional law, are textual.[19]

The better conclusion, at least at this point, is that Justice Thomas's proposal should be evaluated as quite far-reaching, even if limited to the Supreme Court's dealing with its own precedents, and still more so if adopted by the federal courts of appeals and the state judiciaries. But as readers of this book know, the American legal tradition is characterized by change as well as by continuity.

19. On the existence of legitimate forms of constitutional law argument beyond those closely tied to the constitutional text, *see* Powell, *The Practice of American Constitutional Law* 39–43, 203–06.

Additional Reading

The common advice in the 1L year to focus on your assignments rather than look for more to read is generally sound. But the existence of this book proves that, as with almost everything else in the law, there are exceptions, at least in my judgment. The following books will give the reader accessible *and* sophisticated insight into some of the topics we have addressed.

Legal Reasoning

Frederick Schauer, *Thinking Like a Lawyer: A New Introduction to Legal Reasoning* (2012)

Lloyd Weinreb, *Legal Reason: The Use of Analogy in Legal Argument* (2d ed. 2016)

Legal History

Lawrence Friedman, *Law in America: A Short History* (2002)

Law as a Calling

Charles L. Black, Jr., *The Humane Imagination* (1986)

Charles Fried & Gregory Fried, *Because It Is Wrong* (2010)

James Boyd White, *Keep Law Alive* (2019)

Holmes

Thomas Healy, *The Great Dissent: How Oliver Wendell Holmes Changed His Mind—and Changed the History of Free Speech in America* (2014) [There are many biographies of Holmes and several are very good. But this account of how Justice Holmes came to write his famous First Amendment opinion in *Abrams v. United States*, and what came of it later, may be the best introduction to him as a judge.]

The Essential Holmes (Richard A. Posner ed. 1997)

Cardozo

Benjamin N. Cardozo, *The Nature of the Judicial Process* (Andrew L. Kaufman intro. 2010) [The introduction to this edition was written by Cardozo's biographer. When you have more time, consider reading Kaufman's great biography, *Cardozo* (2010).]

Index